The work presented in this report was carried out in the Economics and Statistics Department of the OECD Secretariat in the course of 1987. It was intended as one contribution to the continuing international discussions of ways of strengthening the multilateral surveillance of economic policies, and thereby of improving the performance of both national economies and the international system as a whole. The objective of this particular project was to see what lessons for the future might be learned from an examination of past episodes in which countries were led to make important changes in policies that seemed, for one reason or another, to be proving unsustainable. The exercise covers eleven OECD countries, and the episodes studied lie between the mid-1970s and the mid-1980s.

The project was designed and in large part executed by Stephen Potter, Val Koromzay and Bixio Barenco; important contributions were made by Odile Sallard and Jorgen Elmeskov; and help was also provided by Christian Saint-Etienne and Rick Imai. Acknowledgements are due to a large number of national officials for their comments and suggestions. Nevertheless, views expressed in this report do not necessarily correspond with those of the national authorities concerned; and it is published on the responsibility of the Secretary-General.

Table of contents

Chapter 1

Introduction, summary and conclusions

Introduction

The central question that prompted this study might be put as follows: why do governments act at certain times to alter substantially the course of their macro-economic policies, but not at other times? While this question is one that might be considered interesting at any time, it has in recent years acquired more than academic importance. Particularly since 1985, when the report issued by the Group of Ten on improving the workings of the international monetary system gave particular emphasis to strengthening surveillance over economic policies, the major industrial countries have been engaged in developing a framework for strengthened economic-policy co-operation as a means of achieving greater international monetary and financial stability. If such a process is to "have teeth", it clearly needs to be grounded in what governments are realistically able and willing to do in certain circumstances to redirect their policies so as to deal with domestic or international disturbances; and it seemed natural, in raising this question, to focus in the first instance on what governments actually have done, or not done, in previous situations or "episodes" when pressures built up.

An important concept – though one that is difficult to define precisely – which has shaped the approach to history taken in this study is that of *sustainability*. The premise is that if a given course of policy encounters difficulties, it is because the accumulating evidence suggests that the chosen course is, for one reason or another, unsustainable. The question of when, and how, governments come to recognise a particular situation as unsustainable, and the way such recognition influences subsequent policy choices has been one of the guiding threads in the analysis of the episodes covered by this study.

It is perhaps important to stress at the outset that, by focusing on the issue of sustainability, the selection of episodes for consideration is not a random one. The study has selected episodes where, faced with indications that a situation was unsustainable or threatening to become so, action was taken. Situations which might have appeared to require action, but did not in fact do so because they resolved themselves one way or the other, have therefore not been considered – and this may relativise to some extent the conclusions that can be drawn from this study.

This point is particularly relevant when it comes to a consideration of whether particular economic indicators, or sets of indicators, provided adequate "advance warning" that an unsustainable situation was developing. This study concludes that in most of the episodes considered, such advance warnings were available. But it can be argued with justice that such a conclusion would only be warranted if it could be shown that such indicators were not also giving "advance warnings" in cases where, in fact, policy adjustments were not required.

As regards the methodology adopted in the study of these historical episodes, it might be noted that these accounts contain little in the way of formal analysis, and do not attempt to be historical scholarship in the academic sense of the term. The approach was to write out, for each episode, a rough account based on statistical sources and contemporary published accounts, and then to discuss these with national authorities – including as far as possible those individuals directly involved in providing policy assessment and advice in the period considered. That having been said, the responsibility for what is contained in the various episodes presented in this study lies entirely with the OECD, and not with Member governments. While the study clearly could not have been undertaken without the help that national authorities provided in clarifying the issues and the facts surrounding these episodes, the interpretations and assessments provided are exclusively those of the OECD.

The structure of the study is as follows: the remainder of this Chapter presents an overview of the episodes that have been analysed, and provides an account of the principal conclusions that seem to emerge from them. The episodes themselves are presented – much as individual set-pieces – in the chapters that follow.

Past experience: a summary

An overview of the "historical episodes"

In considering the historical episodes covered in this study, it is important to bear in mind a number of the features of the international economic environment between the mid-1970s and the early-1980s which were affecting virtually all countries. First, countries faced serious inflation problems and slowing productivity growth. Second, there were the disruptive macroeconomic effects of the two oil shocks, as well as their international ramifications. Third, they were having to learn to live with the regime of floating exchange rates, which in some respects turned out to function differently from prior expectations. Fourth, with uncertainty about the role of reserve currencies in the new system, both traditional and emerging reserve currency countries were subject at times to additional pressures. These various features of the international environment sharply increased the degree of uncertainty and greatly complicated the task of the authorities. Many well-established policy rules and associated analytical underpinnings no longer seemed valid. Monetary targeting was adopted, and gave good results in some countries, though it was problematic in others. Policies had to be framed under the pressure of events and in a tentative manner as the authorities sought new points of reference and operational guidelines.

Domestically, many economies were marked in the 1970s by a build-up of rigidities on the supply side, combined with unfulfillable expectations of improving standards of living: this made full employment progressively more difficult to achieve with a tolerable rate of inflation. The share of public spending in GNP tended to rise strongly, as did real labour costs and tax burdens, thereby squeezing profits and discouraging productive investment and job creation.

It was against this kind of background that the three earliest episodes considered unfolded: the weak-currency episodes of 1976 in *Italy* and the *United Kingdom,* and in milder form in *France.* Similar forces were at work in some of the subsequent episodes, including *Germany* in 1980-81. For reasons varying from one episode to another, but ultimately related to socio-political factors, the authorities, although generally aware of the risks involved, used macroeconomic policy to support real demand and incomes even after the terms-of-trade losses due to the oil shocks and the slowdown of world economic growth had occurred. They could not seriously tackle the root causes of their problems until the situation approached crisis conditions and the need for remedial action, on the internal as well as on the external side, became evident and broadly accepted by the unions and the population at large. The climax and the irresistible push to act came with a run on the currency, which raised fears of an uncontrollable spiral between depreciation and inflation. While in these episodes there was probably no dilemma in a fundamental economic sense between internal and external requirements, the deterioration of the balance of payments was typically perceived by the authorities as creating a policy dilemma up to the point where a currency crisis called forth a policy U-turn. But once the fundamental shift of priorities from demand support to the stabilization of the exchange rate and the reduction of inflation had been decided, there was no longer any conflict at a policy level between the dominant internal objective and the external objective, though the need to "play it safe" and rapidly restore external confidence often obliged the authorities to adopt a stronger and faster adjustment than they might have chosen on purely domestic grounds. It seems, however, that macroeconomic policies were deployed more actively than policies to improve the structural functioning of economies. Indeed, new microeconomic distortions and rigidities were sometimes created by measures introduced to obtain short-run relief from macroeconomic pressure. This may help explain why external conditions typically turned around quite rapidly while the correction of internal tensions and imbalances proved a move intractable and longer-term task.

The next group of episodes is centred on the years 1977-79, and involves the *United States* on the one hand and three countries that felt the counterpart of U.S. developments particularly strongly – *Japan, Germany* and *Switzerland* – on the other. On the U.S. side, the episode was marked by an attempt to accelerate economic growth (rather than merely to prevent a slowdown as in the 1976 European episodes). In part this reflected the intellectual climate of the time more generally, as epitomised by the "strategy for sustained economic expansion" adopted by the OECD Ministerial meeting in June 1976 and similar undertakings in other fora; thus Japan and Germany, too, were prepared to agree to expansionary action in 1978 when it became widely accepted that U.S. external difficulties – related to a current-account deficit and the weakening dollar – stemmed partly from slow growth outside the United States. From a purely economic viewpoint, correction of the U.S. situation – especially its domestic aspect – was perhaps easier and the effects more immediate than was the case for the 1976 episodes: disequilibria and tensions were largely concentrated at the macroeconomic level, with structural features playing a secondary role as compared with Europe. Nonetheless, from a political point of view the decision to make a U-turn was probably even more difficult and required mounting external pressure as a trigger – first pressure on the currency (and its reflection in domestic inflation) and later "peer pressure" by foreign monetary authorities as well. The U.S. response came in two phases: a largely foreign-exchange-oriented initiative in late 1978, and a decisive tightening of monetary policy in the face of accelerating inflation a year later. The U.S. authorities were confronted, at times, by something of an internal-external dilemma, even though in the early stages of the episode a decline of the dollar was generally considered appropriate, while towards the end of the episode a monetary tightening was seen as necessary for both internal and external reasons. The United States also (as part of the 1978 Summit package) made the important "supply-side" response of decontrolling oil prices.

Viewed from the other side, the Japanese, German and Swiss episodes of 1977-79 have a number of points in common, notably a sizeable current-account surplus. A peculiarity of the Japanese episode seems to be its degree of over-adjustment, in terms not only of currency appreciation but also of fiscal stimulus, which were both relatively greater than Germany's. The combined effect of the two, however, yielded remarkably steady Japanese output growth. The Swiss episode is a rare example of a near-textbook "dilemma case": an economy in internal equilibrium confronting an acute shock of external origin (the weakness of the dollar). At a certain point, the Swiss authorities' response was to abandon their money targets and give absolute priority to the exchange rate, at the expense of a massive increase in the monetary base, which had subsequently to be unwound. For all three surplus countries, the policy dilemma, largely caused by developments abroad, can be seen as a cost that can arise from participation in an open international economic and financial system – a cost that is liable to be most acute in a small country such as Switzerland, where the benefits of participation in world markets are commensurately greater. In such cases, the best domestic economic policy can do may be to minimise that cost.

Belgium, the *Netherlands* and *Sweden* each had structural problems that built up in the course of the late 1970s. Although each country's situation naturally had its own distinctive features, all three suffered, in varying proportions, from the effects of increasing government involvement in the economy, excessive growth of real wages and loss of international competitiveness. In Sweden, moreover, domestic problems were particularly exacerbated by the slowdown of world economic growth. The need for action was generally recognised at the policy-analytic level of government years before decisive measures were actually taken. In the event, the episode culminated for all three countries in 1982, in each case following a change of government. Sweden and Belgium, which had sizeable current deficits, devalued their currencies. In Sweden this measure was seen as supporting demand and thereby making budget consolidation possible without a violation of the low unemployment target; in Belgium the primary emphasis in the short term was, in conjunction with a reduction of wage indexation, on improving the position of the corporate sector. The Netherlands, which actually had a large current surplus but had experienced simultaneous leaps in the budget deficit and unemployment, made a decisive move towards budgetary consolidation.

The *French* episode of 1982-83 is a striking case of a unilateral attempt to accelerate growth (and enact social programmes and other political commitments such as nationalisation) against a background of slower growth abroad. By this time most countries were adhering to the very different kind of strategy for the medium term that took shape around 1980 in the wake of the second oil shock, and which emphasized control of inflation, budgetary rigour and market-oriented initiatives to improve the functioning of economies. The deterioration of the current account, together with downward pressure on the franc, obliged the authorities in 1983 to devalue and to adopt deflationary policies to bring the French economy more into line with developments abroad. From the viewpoint of the French authorities the episode constituted an acute dilemma situation, arising from goals and policies which were largely out of step with those of their major trading partners. This episode stands out, perhaps with the totally different case of Switzerland, as one of the most vivid examples of how international interdependence can impose limits on governments' freedom of action.

The remaining episode studied for this exercise, *Canada* in the early 1980s, is not one clearly marked by unsustainability. But it is an instructive example of the pressures to act that can arise for a country with very close trading and financial links to a larger neighbour, when shocks (in this case the strongly rising U.S. dollar and high and fluctuating interest rates) emanate from that neighbour. Canada had higher inflation than the United States over the 1981-84 period, and a risk premium emerged on Canadian-dollar-denominated assets. Canada also found itself "mimicking" to some extent the U.S. policy mix; and by the end of the period examined the fiscal deficit was larger than would have been sustainable over the long term.

What was unsustainable?

For the purpose of the present exercise, an "unsustainable" situation can be defined as one which, if left untended, is likely to result in "discontinuities" and dislocations – such as a collapse of the exchange rate and accelerating inflation – with severe costs – economic, political and social. The exact role of the external current account in giving rise to unsustainable situations has been a point of long-standing interest. It is one of the conclusions of this exercise that the current account *as such* seems to have been regarded as the crucial unsustainable element in rather few of the episodes considered, though its indicator role in pointing to fundamental problems was relevant in most of them. On the side of surpluses, the current account was regarded as *politically* unsustainable in Japan in 1978 because of the trade and other international tensions to which it gave rise. On the deficit side, the current account seems to have been the decisive element only in France, though it was one element among several in Sweden, Belgium, Italy and the United Kingdom. In the United States in 1977-78, the current deficit was widely viewed as worrying, a perception which lay behind the strategy of encouraging partner countries to expand demand and allowing the dollar to decline. There were other episodes in which a current deficit was present, but in those cases it tended to be regarded as being of a manageable size and symptomatic of difficulties in the domestic economy rather than a problem in its own right.

Closely related to the current account, *external indebtedness* seems to have been, if not unsustainable, at least a key constraining element in France (where this became a politically sensitive variable) and Italy (which effectively lost access temporarily to international credit markets). For both countries, these were rather surprising developments; neither of them had been anything like so indebted in relative terms as, for example, some of the smaller OECD countries.

Also current-account related, *loss of international competitiveness* resulting from steeply appreciating currencies that were the counterpart of dollar weakness was the key element of unsustainability in 1977-78 for Japan, Germany and Switzerland. Had they continued, such losses would have placed intolerable strains on the tradeables sectors of these economies and portended unacceptable current-account deficits.

At least with the benefit of hindsight, *inflation* was the crucial unsustainable feature of developments in the United States in 1977-79, attempts to maintain rapid growth encountering capacity limits sooner than expected; it was recognition of this that resulted in decisive action. Rapid inflation was also the major unsustainable aspect of the complexes of economic problems experienced by the United Kingdom and Italy in the mid-1970s and, to a much lesser degree, by Germany in 1980-81.

Those *complexes of problems* included rigidities and imbalances in the domestic real economy (reflected notably in excessive real wage increases and the squeeze on profits); unsustainably large budget deficits and a rapidly rising share of government spending in GNP; and an erosion of international competitiveness. As already noted, it was an interacting set of problems of this kind that underlay also the gradual drift towards unsustainable situations in Belgium, the Netherlands and Sweden.

Why was corrective action delayed?

One of the motivations behind this exercise was to throw light on the role and use of indicators. It is a – perhaps surprising – general finding from the episodes examined that the lack of early warnings or leading indicators does not seem to have played an important part. In most cases, even without a formal system of indicators, the "writing was on the wall": a combination of the usual economic data and mainstream economic analysis provided the authorities with fair warning of potential trouble ahead. But policy responses were in many cases slow: for most of the episodes considered, there was a lag of something between several months and several years between identification at the policy-analytic level of likely problems and the formulation of a policy response. Of course, it would always have been useful to have *more* accurate and timely gauges of the build-up of pressure and imbalances. But given the constraints under which the authorities were typically operating, it seems doubtful whether better indicators, by themselves, would have significantly changed the process of policy formulation or the unfolding of the episodes.

Two general and two more specific qualifications might be made to this conclusion. First, there is likely to be an element of hindsight in the assessment of these episodes which makes the "writing on the wall" seem clearer than it actually was and understates the degree of uncertainty which surrounded these developments. While this, to a certain extent, may be unavoidable, a review of analyses written at the time – notably the OECD Country Surveys – generally confirms that the elements for detecting emerging problems were indeed available in advance. Second, by including only problem situations this selection of episodes is in fact biased, and a full sample might show instances where the indicators were misleading in pointing to cases of unsustainability which did not materialise.

The first more specific qualification is that indicators were not all giving the same message. In the episodes considered, the most timely and useful warnings typically came from cost-price data – and occasionally the real exchange rate – as well as monetary aggregates. In the United States and Canada, however, financial innovation and other factors destabilized the demand for money, making interpretation of the monetary aggregates difficult (a problem that was to become more widespread later). The current account and even trade figures, while frequently conveying useful contemporaneous information, were not always a reliable leading indicator, and the nominal exchange rate was often deceptively stable until the outbreak of a crisis.

Second, heavily adjusted or derived estimates seem at times to have misled the authorities or delayed recognition of problems. Undue adjustment of, for example, inflation numbers for "special factors" can obscure an emerging adverse trend – and may indeed have done so for a time in the United States in 1977-78. Most significantly, perhaps, estimates (by national authorities as well as by international organisations) of potential output growth and of the margin of economic slack now seem to have been too optimistic in many countries in the second half of the 1970s. As a result, it seems likely in several cases that countries ran more expansionary policies, sometimes partly as a result of peer pressure, than they would have done with the benefit of hindsight. And estimates for other "derived" concepts that depend on a notion of potential output may in turn have been misleading: "structural" budget balances, for example, were typically in worse shape than they appeared to be at the time. These issues were appreciated, and their implications understood, relatively early in the Netherlands.

If the absence of advance warnings was, by and large, *not* the reason for the delay in taking necessary policy action in past episodes, what was the explanation? There seems generally to have been a mixture of reasons, which can be grouped under two broad heads: prevailing economic ideas and views; and political factors.

Although neo-classical and monetarist ideas were well-established by the mid-1970s, actual policy-making in many countries continued to be much influenced by the *ideas and views* around which a broad consensus had developed during the 1960s. Thus, there was thought to be an exploitable trade-off between inflation and unemployment; the efficacy of incomes policy in a situation of strong demand pressures was over-estimated in some countries; and the power of demand management policies was often exaggerated, with the result that supply-side or microeconomic considerations were neglected.

Floating exchange rates had been incorporated in policy makers' thinking, but not always appropriately: in some countries, too much weight was placed on the hoped-for removal of the external constraint with floating rates, and not enough on the need to provide a nominal "anchor" for policies and expectations domestically now that the fixed-exchange-rate anchor had gone. Although much discussed, the potential dangers of floating – the risk either of a vicious circle between depreciation and inflation or of a spiral between appreciation and the current-account surplus in nominal terms (due to J-curves) – may not have been fully perceived in the early phases of some of the episodes.

These remarks are not intended to be critical; they are made with the benefit of hindsight. As noted above, these were difficult times for economic policy. There was naturally a reluctance to abandon ideas and approaches that had served well – or had seemed to do so – over a substantial period. Thus, a number of countries' episodes are a history of the gradual acceptance of the need for a strong commitment to low inflation, and for the key role of credible monetary policy in achieving it; for more realistic approaches to incomes policy, geared to needed adjustment of real wages and profits; for curbing excessive growth of government spending; and for pursuing fiscal policy with regard to its effects on expectations and the growth of public debt. Viewed in relation to the history of economics and economic systems, these were not new discoveries, but in large part a resurrection of earlier conventional wisdom.

Even in a period when a government is not faced with the problems of internalising new ideas and getting them accepted by the population at large, *political factors* will inevitably tend to delay needed economic policy action. Economic matters have naturally to compete with many others for the limited time of governments, and the launching of a new initiative may require an appropriate "occasion"; the authorities and the general public are more impressed by hard facts than by analysis and forecasts that suggest that the situation is liable to deteriorate – and it is anyway rare for a forecast to depict a disastrously worsening outcome; and unpleasant measures have to be negotiated with the relevant constituencies. For all these reasons, while it may be excessive to conclude that industrial democracies are better at overcoming crises than at preventing them, deteriorating situations may drift for some time, with the risk of tensions and imbalances approaching unsustainable levels. The following section discusses the factors that brought drifting situations to a climax where action *was* taken.

What triggered a policy response?

In almost all the episodes considered, it was *exchange-rate pressure* that brought matters to a head and determined the timing of the introduction of comprehensive policy measures. This happened because, beyond a certain point, the authorities of countries with a weakening currency could no longer tolerate the inflation implications (and reached the limit to which they were willing or able to carry on losing reserves or incurring foreign indebtedness to support the currency), while those with appreciating currencies were not prepared indefinitely to allow an ever-increasing squeeze on their tradeables sectors (or could no longer accept the monetary implications of intervention to limit the currency's rise).

Only in the Netherlands does exchange-market pressure appear to have been absent in the push to take policy action. The policy response in the U.S. episode was in two stages: the package of November 1978 was largely oriented to foreign exchange markets, and was clearly triggered by pressure on the dollar; the shift to tighter monetary policy and new operating procedures in October 1979 was probably triggered more by domestic pressures to fight inflation, but here too exchange-market pressure – as well as foreign peer pressure – played an important part. For the other nine countries, exchange-rate pressure was a major influence, at least as regards timing, and in many cases it was the crucial one.

Mention has already been made of the importance both of new ideas and of political will. It is noticeable that in a majority of the episodes considered the corrective action was taken shortly after the installation of a *new government* or the appointment of a key senior policy maker. Peer pressure from abroad was also important in a number of episodes; in the United Kingdom and Italy it took the institutionalised form of an IMF programme.

What was the nature of the policy response?

Dramatic and consequential as they sometimes were, developments in exchange markets typically were largely symptoms. The fundamental causes of the pressures were either developments in the domestic economy or, more rarely, developments abroad. With the sole exception of Switzerland, therefore, countries' measures taken in response to exchange-rate pressure had to be complemented by policies to correct imbalances of domestic origin.

In all but two cases (Germany in 1980-81 and the Netherlands), the policy response included direct exchange-rate measures: actual devaluations in the context of European fixed parity or "basket" arrangements in France, Belgium and Sweden, where the current account was problematic; more generally, exchange-market intervention or international financing arrangements to finance deficits for an interim period. In all cases, the response included macroeconomic policy measures (indeed, this was almost the criterion of selection for the episodes). The measures were mainly monetary in the United States, Canada and Switzerland, largely fiscal (accompanied in some cases by monetary measures) elsewhere. An important element in some cases was a modification of incomes policy arrangements to promote downward adjustment of real wages: measures taken in France, the United Kingdom, Italy and Belgium had the effect of reducing the degree of indexation in wage formation. Exchange controls were relied upon extensively in the early stages both in deficit and surplus countries to counter mounting pressure on the currency. At best they provided a breathing space, and when conditions reached a climax and the *causes* of the problem were finally tackled they were progressively phased out.

In virtually all cases, the macroeconomic measures ultimately taken seem to have been relatively well-adapted to the circumstances, or were at least regarded as being so by the exchange markets. Although the measures taken could not always be said to be sufficient to put economies back clearly on to a sustainable path, and therefore sometimes needed to be followed up by further action, in no case did a new crisis erupt within the first year or so of the measures having been taken.

Some conclusions and implications for the surveillance of economic policies

Selected conclusions for economic policy

For OECD countries the last decade or so has witnessed a move from the pursuit of a "strategy for growth" to a medium-term strategy based on macroeconomic stability and reinvigoration of the supply side. Since a considerable amount of work already exists on this reorientation of economic policy, the summary here concentrates on more specific lessons in policy areas which seem to emerge from the study of the episodes.

17

One clear lesson is the importance for countries of *paying due attention to developments and policies abroad*. The majority of the situations considered were, or would if left untended have become, unsustainable in their own domestic terms – although it is hardly possible in today's world to visualise any national situation in a purely closed-economy context. But many of the cases considered, and more particularly perhaps the United States and counterpart country episodes in 1977-79 and the French experience in 1982-83, bear eloquent witness to the realities of interdependence: what is sustainable can depend on what is happening abroad. This conclusion should not be thought of merely as expressing the constraints on national performance; it can in principle be built on to devise internationally-co-operative sets of policies for a better (and sustainable) global outcome.

Another lesson suggested by several episodes (the United States, the United Kingdom, Italy and France) is the *difficulty of engineering a depreciation* in a floating regime without the process getting out of hand, especially for a reserve-currency country. More generally, both appreciations and depreciations tended to acquire a momentum of their own – it would seem that there is an extrapolative element in expectations that can gain force over time. In the face of strong expectations of sizeable exchange-rate movements, monetary policy and interest rates became increasingly unable to affect international capital movements and hence exchange rates. To regain a handle on the situation in such circumstances, the authorities needed to give the market an anchor, that is a clear and reliable idea of future exchange-rate developments. The extreme example of success in such an endeavour was the introduction of an explicit exchange-rate ceiling in the Swiss episode. Along similar lines, the Japanese episodes illustrates how, when expectations and exchange-rate changes are driven by the current-account position expressed in nominal terms (with J-curve effects initially obscuring the real adjustment), the result may be a spiral whose effect is to prolong the period of correction and drive the exchange rate to unrealistic levels from which it is then likely to retreat abruptly. In the absence of strong multilateral commitments to exchange-rate stability, and to the policies that would underpin it, it is uncertain how far a country could or should try to stabilize its exchange rate. While for a country like Switzerland it was feasible to tie its currency to the DM, it might not have been feasible (or desirable) for a country like Japan to tie its currency to the dollar.

A closely-related matter is the *credibility* of policy. National authorities often refer to its importance, though different people may have different notions of what credibility involves. Among those examined, the clearest case of a country *having* credibility was Switzerland, where the authorities were able temporarily to abandon a well-established approach and pursue another, completely at variance with it, without adverse market reactions; their ability to do so was no doubt attributable to their

18

successful record in achieving the final objective of price stability. More generally, it was a frequent conclusion that credibility was difficult to acquire, easy to lose and never to be taken for granted.

One aspect of insufficient credibility is the *risk premium* embodied in a nation's interest rates. This was an important issue at one time or another in a number of the countries considered. In particular, it importantly influenced perceptions of the potential costs of using currency devaluation, rather than restraining domestic costs, as a means of counteracting a deterioration in external competitiveness. In the Netherlands, where the hard-currency option was adopted, possible short-term gains in competitiveness brought about by devaluation were judged to be outweighed by the persistently higher interest rates that would be needed to compensate investors for the perceived risk that one devaluation could be followed by others. This consideration also played an important part in the progressive shift in French policy thinking away from the notion that losses in competitiveness could be systematically offset by periodic devaluations. Even in Sweden, where a large devaluation was decided upon, risk premium considerations meant that the authorities would not consider a policy of smaller but repeated or periodic devaluations as sustainable. It is more difficult to assess the role of such risk premia in the case of countries whose exchange rates are not pegged – though it seems that Canadian interest rates embodied a risk premium relative to U.S. rates in the early 1980s because of the periodic bouts of weakness of the Canadian dollar. Finally, it might be noted that risk premia cannot always be avoided by pegging: indeed, in the absence of full credibility that a parity will under no circumstances be altered, market perceptions that an exchange rate is "out of line" can generate large capital outflows and require higher interest rates to avoid currency depreciation.

Turning to the *announcement of policy objectives,* the experience suggests that it is generally more advisable for targets to relate to variables that are under the authorities' control, or nearly so, than to final objectives for growth or employment, although – as noted – monetary targeting has at times itself been subject to problems. The Japanese episode is a particularly instructive case of the problems that can arise with a commitment to a real growth target – rather than to a specified degree of policy action. Simple *rules of thumb* were found useful in some cases: in France, the ceiling of 3 per cent of GDP for the budget deficit was helpful in putting together a framework for austerity measures and in sensitising public opinion; in Japan the 30 per cent norm for the budget deficit in relation to government spending for a time provided a useful discipline on spending; in the Netherlands the 4 per cent norm for the structural budget deficit in relation to net national income may also have been useful in shaping the policy debate.

Some particular considerations attached to *reserve-currency countries*. The weakness of the dollar in 1977-79 was thought to be exacerbated by "currency substitution", that is, the reduction of the proportion of dollar assets in official reserves of a number of countries. The accumulation of sterling balances by some OPEC countries for a time in the wake of the first oil shock reduced the pressure on the United Kingdom to adjust, thereby making the ultimate adjustment all the more painful. The German episode of 1980-81 can be read as evidence that a second-line reserve currency is in an especially vulnerable and asymmetrical position because funds may flow in when the dominant reserve currency is in trouble and flow out again as soon as it recovers – to some extent irrespective of the economic performance of the second-line reserve-currency country; meanwhile, funds will also be liable to flow out in a massive way whenever the second line reserve-currency country itself shows signs of trouble.

Relevance to the present "episode"

The rise and fall of the dollar over the period 1981 to 1988 will be a rich episode for future historians. It was not included in the present exercise on the same footing as the other episodes because the necessary sense of perspective would have been difficult to achieve, and because its final resolution cannot yet be clearly discerned. Before discussing implications for the future, however, it is worth considering briefly what is new and what is familiar in this episode.

There are a number of important new features:

- The sheer size of the swings in the dollar – in nominal as well as in real terms – and of the current-account imbalances of the United States, Japan and Germany;
- The fact that a widening U.S. current deficit was for several years accompanied by an appreciating dollar;
- Partly related, the fact that a large current deficit was not accompanied by an intensifying inflation problem in the United States;
- At least over the period 1981-85, the greater international differences of view than earlier about important economic mechanisms and inter-relationships;
- That the U.S. current deficit cumulated over several years to a huge figure without there having been any serious concern about "currency substitution".

Taken together, this is an impressive list: it is no exaggeration to describe this episode as unprecedented. First, in terms of size, the U.S. current-account deficit and the Japanese surplus have exceeded 2½ per cent of GNP for four years already (1984-87), and are projected to continue at around this level for another year or more.

Since 1960, no major OECD country had ever experienced a current-account imbalance of this size for more than two years in a row. Second, as for the nature of the imbalances, a number of interrelated factors – including high U.S. real interest rates, confidence in U.S. monetary policy and in the economy in general, and an OECD-wide trend towards liberalisation of both domestic and cross-border financial transactions – have resulted in a rather inhabitual role for international capital movements. While, in the past, financial flows tended to follow and amplify current-account imbalances, this time they preceded and – through the appreciation of the dollar – to a large extent *caused* the U.S. current-account deficit. Even after the turnaround of the dollar, international capital movements continued for a couple of years to provide the necessary financing in a remarkably smooth way. These trends, especially at their onset, were certainly awkward ones to assess, and views concerning the economic mechanisms at work and their sustainability diverged significantly. Finally, with respect to the appropriate policy response, the fact that this time, unlike practically all previous cases of external deficits, inflation is not a major problem calls for a gradual correction of the U.S. current-account deficit in a context of continued economic growth. But this approach, which has never been successfully implemented before and may carry the risk of a policy dilemma for the U.S. authorities, has caused some misgivings, especially outside the United States.

At the same time, however, the episode had some family resemblances to earlier ones, and like them it was susceptible of economic analysis. For example, the OECD was by 1982 suggesting that the dollar would decline (while recognising that it might first have further to rise); and by 1983 the term "unsustainable" was being applied to the prevailing pattern of exchange rates, and by implication to the emerging pattern of payments balances. (Other international staffs were making similar analyses.) The timing was of course not captured correctly, but a long "advance warning" was sounded.

Furthermore, without wishing to suggest that a study of the earlier episodes would have been an adequate preparation for this one, it is worth pointing out a number of respects in which earlier experience was at least of some relevance. These include:

- The problems of an economy growing for a prolonged period at a rate substantially faster in relation to productive potential than the average of partner countries, even allowing for its capacity to gain foreign markets through productivity gains, innovation and marketing success (several earlier episodes);
- The difficulty of engineering a controlled depreciation (several earlier episodes);

21

- The emergence of risk premia in countries' interest rates (a number of earlier episodes);
- The implications for monetary control of exchange-market intervention in appreciating countries (Germany and Switzerland in 1978);
- The inadequacy of foreign exchange measures alone and the need for them to be backed up by appropriate macroeconomic policy adjustments (several episodes, but notably the United States in 1978-79).

Implications for multilateral surveillance

One of the main objects of this exercise was to determine ways in which the inputs to policy making might be improved, with a view in turn to improving economic performance. The national experiences compiled for this purpose provide clues as to where things went wrong in the past and where to seek improvements in the future. The OECD's reading of those experiences is that there is no royal road to more effective policy surveillance: it is a case of looking carefully at each of the stages in the process and attempting to make whatever improvements are feasible wherever there may be scope for them.

In drawing the implications for surveillance, a first question may concern the *level of ambition* that is appropriate. Recent international discussions of surveillance or of indicators have regularly concluded that "fine-tuning" and "automaticity" were inappropriate. In other words, a degree of departure from a desired path should be tolerated, and not give rise to attempts at correction. But refraining from action for too long is precisely what may allow an "unsustainable" or crisis situation to emerge. Although such situations can be salutary in provoking adoption of better policies, the premise of recent attempts to improve surveillance is that countries consider it desirable for corrective action to be taken before such a situation is reached. Hence, efforts should be aimed at improving the timeliness of action taken to avert unsustainable situations. One area where improvements stand to be made is in *speeding-up the political recognition* of the need (when it exists) for action. This is where delays have typically been longest in the past. Progress here will inevitably be largely a domestic matter for each country. But it could be that improvements under some of the other heads below would be helpful here too; and international peer pressure might have a stronger role to play.

The first step in a surveillance process is *economic analysis*. While the general conclusion of this study is that failure to recognise worsening situations at the analytical level has not been the crucial element delaying corrective action in the past, there is always scope to do better. There has been much stress recently on enhancing the

22

use of *indicators*, on which some conclusions have been put forward above. The OECD's assessment is that aspects of economies that are particularly difficult to capture in summary indicators are *monetary policy and conditions* and the *supply side*. The former has been made especially difficult by continuing financial innovation. For the latter, a specific issue is the role of estimates of *potential output*. This is a difficult concept to define precisely or measure reliably – and its over-estimation was a source of problems in a number of the episodes examined. (For the period ahead there seems some risk that it may be being under-estimated.) At the same time, some such indicator of the likely growth of supply is hard to do without.

As regards the surveillance of *individual country* situations, the impression from the present exercise is that although a number of common themes and patterns emerge from the past episodes, each one is strongly coloured by its own time and place. In other words, if surveillance is to be strengthened there is probably no alternative to a case-by-case approach, exploring country situations in some depth.

However, it may be important for surveillance of individual national economies to be supplemented by analysis of their combined performance as a group: too little attention was probably paid in the second half of the 1970s to the sustainability of the growth of the *OECD or world economy as a whole* that was resulting from the policy approach of the time. Interest has indeed been expressed recently in developing the analysis (and indicators) of the state or policy stance of the global economy, or that of the major countries taken together.

As regards the surveillance of *international interactions and policy compatibility*, this exercise in itself has little to contribute, at least not directly since the aim was not to focus on this question. But such interactions certainly did exist in practically all episodes and are often referred to explicitly in the individual country chapters that follow; and certain episodes were defined above as being largely the "counterpart of each other". Moreover, much work currently done at the OECD is aimed at this question. For example, the OECD has recently enriched its traditional analysis by embodying medium-term internationally-linked policy scenarios. It seems, indeed, to be particularly important to inject more forward-looking material into the surveillance process in the form of short- and especially medium-term projections (in, of course, an internationally-agreed analytical framework).

Reference was made above to the difficulties arising, over the 1981-85 period, from differences in countries' *ideas and views* on economic policy. Although there now seems again to be a greater degree of consensus, such differences remain an inevitable source of possible problems. Peer pressure is fully effective only if the peers share a broadly agreed view of the objectives to be pursued, and the way in which the economic system works. One of the purposes of multilateral surveillance is to enable

23

divergent perceptions to be articulated, compared and reviewed, with a view to reconciling or at any rate clarifying differences.

A related question is whether there are *new features of the 1980s* that substantially modify the conclusions that can be drawn from the past. The key new feature seems to be the rapid growth of the international financial markets at a time when the main national markets are effectively liberalised – potentially as significant a development as the move in the 1970s to flexible exchange rates. The experience of the United States in 1981-85 illustrates the kind of situation that can arise in this new world. That fiscal expansion (coupled with monetary restraint) would go together with currency *appreciation* was a well established text-book result (associated with Mundell and Fleming), but one whose practical relevance was widely doubted and which, when it actually occurred, was highly disconcerting to policy makers outside the United States. The difficulty in such circumstances of accepting that a widening current-account deficit in the United States was evidence of trouble ahead, at a time when the dollar was still appreciating and domestic inflation apparently well under control, is certainly understandable. But it underlines the need for multilateral surveillance to be based on a complete and forward-looking analysis of a situation – and for that analysis to be based on agreed foundations.

It could be that the United States is an extreme case in its ability to attract capital inflows; but it would appear useful anyway for more thinking to be done on the implications for multilateral surveillance of a world in which for many countries a possible constraint on realisable capital flows may have given place to a creditworthiness constraint related to stocks of debt, i.e. a constraint that may be rather loose for a considerable period, but then tighten abruptly at a moment that can hardly be foreseen. In such a financially liberalised world different countries are likely to be affected differently, and the task of multilateral surveillance to provide early warnings may be both more difficult and more important.

Chapter 2

United States, 1977-79:
facing up to inflation

Introduction

This chapter focuses on economic and policy developments in the United States over the period 1977 through 1979 – a period that began with a strong policy emphasis on achieving high growth, was punctuated by the "free fall" of the dollar in the second half of 1978, and ended with the adoption by the Federal Reserve of a new operating procedure for the conduct of monetary policy and a significant tightening to bring down inflation, at the risk (subsequently realised) of recession.

The broad policy context might be summarised under the following six headings:

a)   The new Administration of President Carter came into office in the second year following the "oil shock" recession of 1974-75, with a commitment to accelerate the pace of recovery towards full capacity utilisation. Indeed, the commitment to strong growth was not only a domestic priority but part of a global strategy for growth which the new Administration promoted from the beginning. (Somewhat later this strategy came to be dubbed the "locomotive theory".)

b)   Inflation, which had come down markedly in the 1985 recession to below 6 per cent in 1976, was viewed by the Administration as being driven by a wage-price spiral that could not be unwound rapidly at acceptable costs. The "sacrifice ratio" (the amount of foregone output needed to reduce inflation by 1 per cent) was considered high enough to all but foreclose the option of using restrictive policy as a means of reducing inflation. Thus, while inflation was an Administration concern from the beginning, the policy instruments mobilised to deal with it were limited to those that would not adversely affect output. The objective was to achieve a gradual deceleration by avoiding economic overheating, and by influencing the wage-price spiral directly through guidelines, tax incentives and structural policies that would generate favourable "price shocks" within the economy by reducing costs or increasing competition. In practice, guidelines were progressively strengthened over the period, at least in intent, though Congress generally failed to pass measures such as the proposed tax-based incomes policy (TIP) that would have given this programme more teeth. And as regards structural policies, alongside important successes (such as airline deregulation), there were also a number of countervailing actions (increases in minimum wages and agricultural price-support levels) that tended to work in the opposite direction;

c) The new Administration also perceived reducing demand for imported oil as a major priority. Numerous measures to promote alternative energy supplies and encourage conservation were adopted, but the deregulation of crude oil prices proved to be a politically intractable issue with Congress because of the large inter-regional income transfers associated with decontrol and conflicting interests concerning how these transfers could be taxed. A process of decontrol was finally set in train in the Summer of 1979;

d) Fiscal policy was moderately expansionary in intent, with a discretionary easing introduced in 1977, and a further tax cut signed into law in late 1978, to take effect in 1979. In both cases, however, the actions finally taken were scaled back relative to initial announced intentions – reflecting uncertainty on the amount of fiscal stimulus that was appropriate, but also conveying to markets a perception that policy lacked "consistency". *Ex post*, fiscal policy during this period moved in a moderately restrictive direction, with federal expenditures falling slightly as a share of GNP, and the tax share rising – so that the Federal deficit fell from 3.9 per cent of GNP in 1976 to 1.2 per cent in 1979, before widening again under the impact of the 1980 recession. The reasons for the discrepancy between intent and outturn are difficult to pin down precisely. Fiscal drag and lagging expenditures in the face of stronger-than-anticipated growth in nominal GNP may be partial explanations;

e) Monetary policy was in principle defined in terms of an M1 target range, though it seems clear that reasonable stability of short-term interests rates was an important objective of the monetary authorities. While in 1976 stable short-term interest rates had been consistent with achieving the money-growth target (reflecting in part an apparently exogenous acceleration in velocity), in succeeding years monetary targets were generally overshot despite rising interest rates, and these overshootings were accepted in the sense that targets for succeeding years were anchored in actual outturns rather than the previous year's target ("base drift"). More fundamentally, the objective of the monetary authorities was to achieve a gradual deceleration of inflation ("bending inflation down") rather than to adopt clearly restrictive policies that might threaten recovery. Particularly since internal forecasts (at least in the early part of this period) tended consistently to show inflation peaking in the current quarter and then decelerating, the case for stronger anti-inflation actions remained moot for some considerable time;

f) As regards the dollar exchange rate, the Administration, like its predecessor, initially held the view that intervention should be limited to "countering disorderly market conditions". By early 1978, however, attitudes had begun to change and a somewhat more activist intervention policy, including co-ordinated actions with other monetary authorities, was pursued. Clearly by 1979, and perhaps earlier, more fundamental questions about the role of the dollar in the International Monetary System were being asked within the Administration, and it seriously explored the idea of a Substitution Account as a means of addressing what had come to be seen as the problem of the "dollar overhang".

The episode

At the start of 1977 the case for accelerating the recovery appeared to be a good one. Inflation, as measured by the Consumer Price index, had been steady at below 5 per cent in the second half of 1986; substantial slack remained in the economy, with unemployment seemingly stuck at just below 8 per cent – close to 3 percentage points above the pre-oil shock peak; and growth had decelerated through 1976, ending in a relatively weak quarter. A tax-cut stimulus was proposed by the Administration but then, with evidence that a strong first-quarter rebound was occurring and with a jump in the inflation rate in January-February, this programme was scaled back in subsequent messages to Congress.

Growth was strong in 1977 (averaging 5.5 per cent for the year), unemployment came down by 1 percentage point (in the face of rapid labour-force growth) and inflation – though on average 2 percentage points higher in 1977 than in 1976 – seemed to be generally stable or declining after the "bad months" at the beginning of the year.

One issue of considerable preoccupation was the current account which moved strongly into deficit during 1977 reflecting a relatively strong dollar over the 1975-76 period, rapidly rising oil imports, and the continuing strength of the recovery in the

United States in the face of what was perceived to be a marked slowdown in the rest of the world after the first quarter of 1977. This concern was amplified by internal projections which suggested that the deficit would, in the absence of a weaker dollar or much stronger growth abroad, continue to widen into the indefinite future. These circumstances provoked the statement by Secretary of the Treasury Blumenthal at the June OECD Ministerial and September IMF Governing Board meetings that surplus countries should expand more rapidly or else see their currencies appreciate. Markets interpreted these statements as suggesting that the Administration sought a weaker dollar, and indeed the dollar came under downward pressure in the fall of 1977, depreciating by about 4 per cent in effective terms from September to December, despite rising intervention by other countries, and some limited intervention by the Fed, to stem the decline.

The economic climate deteriorated in 1978. Inflation accelerated markedly in the beginning of the year, and the continuing fall of the dollar, while accepted for a time as necessary to promote external adjustment, was also increasingly a matter of concern because of its expected negative effect on inflation. Macroeconomic policies remained expansionary in intent (including a proposed further tax cut for fiscal year 1979), but the discount rate was raised in January (by $\frac{1}{2}$ percentage point) explicitly on international grounds. Subsequent discount-rate adjustments in May, July, August, September and October were also, at least in part, a response to dollar weakness – though high inflation and continued strong growth argued in the same direction. In March 1978, a joint declaration by the Secretary of the Treasury and the German Finance Minister emphasized the commitment to avoiding disorderly market conditions, and the taking of actions on both sides to promote current-account adjustment. In April the Treasury announced a programme of regular gold sales – in large part as a means of taking some pressure off the trade balance. Market reaction to these measures was generally sceptical, but in the May-July period the dollar did recover for a time and exchange-market conditions stabilized in the face of rising U.S. interest rates and a roughly parallel widening of interest differentials in favour of the dollar. Anticipation of a favourable outcome from the Bonn Summit, including commitments to stronger growth abroad and firm action to curtail oil imports into the United States, may also have contributed to supporting the dollar during this period. Indeed the current-account deficit was already falling in the second quarter, though data on this was not yet available. But bad inflation numbers, a perception of disarray within the Administration, and a concern that the Federal Reserve under its new Chairman G. William Miller would be reluctant to raise interest rates further (the markets had perceived the quarter-point July rise in the discount rate as disappointingly small) combined to lead to a renewal of downward pressure on the dollar in August.

Speculation against the dollar gathered momentum through September and October, reaching a crisis point toward the end of the month. On 24th October President Carter made a major speech outlining a new anti-inflation policy operating through strengthened wage-price guidelines. This lacked credibility in the markets and in the following week the dollar, which had already fallen by over 10 per cent in effective terms since the beginning of the year, plummeted by an additional 3¹/₂ per cent in disorderly conditions.

On 1st November, the Administration and the Fed – in close consultation with the monetary and financial authorities of Germany, Japan and Switzerland – took decisive action to stop the dollar fall. The discount rate was raised by an unprecedented 1 percentage point (to 9¹/₂ per cent), supplementary reserve requirements against large time deposits were imposed on banks, and actions were announced to raise a "war chest" of $ 30 billion in foreign exchange to provide the ammunition for concerted intervention on a large scale. An important part of this package was the announcement that the U.S. government would engage in foreign-currency borrowing ("Carter Bonds") as a means of increasing its foreign exchange holdings. The dollar rebounded immediately on the news, and continued to strengthen for some time in the face of aggressive dollar purchases by the Fed and other major central banks (some $ 13 billion in the space of two months). Generally calmer exchange-market conditions became established by the turn of the year (after some "testing" of the new policy in December). Trade data confirming that the U.S. current-account deficit was being eliminated may also have contributed to dollar stabilization in early 1979.

By the beginning of 1979, dealing with inflation had become the declared number one priority of the Administration (indeed, it was already hotly argued within the Administration in October 1978 whether the tax cut passed by Congress for FY 1979 should not be vetoed, in the interests of a more restrictive fiscal stance). Growth was projected to slow below potential, and this was accepted as it would contribute to reducing inflation, and a restrictive budget was announced for fiscal year 1980. Market interest rates had come down slightly from their November 1978 peak, and were held steady in the first half of 1979 (the Federal Funds rate remaining just over 10 per cent). The persistence of an inverted yield curve during this period may have been taken as an indication of tight monetary conditions and market complacency about inflation. The stability of the dollar (it appreciated slowly over this period in effective terms, being steady against the DM and appreciating against the yen, which was under pressure because of the unfolding of the second oil-price shock) may also have been reassuring. But the money supply – after a brief slowdown in the first months of the year – began to accelerate again and was once again above target ranges. At the same time inflation had clearly ratcheted up again into the double-digit range. This acceleration was much broader and larger than could be attributed to the impact of higher oil prices. Thus real interest rates became increasingly negative; and as interest rates abroad were rising, the interest differential in favour of the dollar was eroding rapidly.

After mid-year 1979 the dollar came under pressure again, particularly *vis-à-vis* the DM. At this time G. William Miller was named to take over as Secretary of the Treasury, and Paul Volcker replaced him as Chairman of the Fed. In the following months – against a background of considerable financial market turmoil, a fall of the dollar *vis-à-vis* the Deutschemark back toward the October 1978 "crisis" level, and mounting foreign criticism of U.S. policy for not being sufficiently anti-inflationary – a plan to revise the operating procedures for the conduct of monetary policy was developed, and announced by Chairman Volcker on 6th October. By shifting from the federal funds rate to non-borrowed reserves as the principal instrument of monetary control, substantially greater short-term flexibility in the movement of the federal funds rate became possible. The changeover to the new procedures was calibrated to assure an initial very strong rise in the federal funds rate (which moved up over 250 basis points in October). Furthermore, the new procedures were keyed to achieving a closer control over the money supply, with a concomitant strengthened determination to achieving money growth within the target ranges.

Initial market reactions to the 6th October announcement were somewhat confused. It took some time before the implications of the change became apparent – and indeed before the markets were convinced that a real change had taken place. The credibility of the new procedures did, however, become established in the narrow sense that "above-target" money stock announcements began to generate immediate rises in short-term rates in anticipation that reserve provision by the Fed would be reduced. Achieving "credibility" in the larger sense of convincing markets that monetary policy was henceforth firmly and durably embarked on a non-inflationary course was, of course, a larger enterprise that extended over the next several years (and the mini-recession of 1980 and the more serious one of 1982).

Main policy considerations

While questions about the U.S. current account, the value of the dollar, and energy policy were of major concern to the Administration at various points during this period, it was the domestic inflation problem that, progressively, became the overriding issue. Yet it was only in late-1979, when inflation was running at over 13 per cent, that this issue was tackled head on. By then, it had become clear that action had been too long deferred. Though more difficult to assess, it does seem that

30

some warning lights were available that, if they had been heeded, might have prompted an earlier response.

- While inflation rose from 1976 to 1977, the consumer price numbers coming in after the strong blip in January and February were not alarming and showed, if anything a tendency towards deceleration below the 6 per cent rate that was then generally regarded as tolerable. With unemployment levels still well above current estimates of the "natural rate", there seemed little objective basis for seeing a conflict between strong recovery and gradual further disinflation. It was only the incoming data for early 1978 that clearly revealed the rising trend of inflation, and even then this could be explained for a while as the result of a sharp run-up in food prices. Indeed, the practice during this period of decomposing price changes into "special factors" and the "underlying rate" may have delayed recognition of the inflation problem relative to a more straightforward approach to measurement;

- Perhaps a central problem was that of a too-optimistic view of the rate of growth of economic potential. At the time a range of estimates for potential output growth were available, and the Administration opted for an estimate near the upper end of the range – and well above what subsequently turned out to be the case. As a result, Administration projections under-estimated the growth of the employment/output ratio during the recovery, and the extent to which wage increases fed through into higher production costs. Yet the evidence of this error became clear only during the course of 1978, in part because initial statistics on labour productivity were much more favourable than emerged from the revised statistics. By then, a good deal of inflationary momentum had already been injected into the economy;

- As regards monetary policy, the persistent overshooting of targets from 1977 onward may have been an indication of excessive ease. But there were countervailing considerations: financial innovation was expected to disturb the money-income relationship. At the same time, the restrictive impact of rising nominal interest rates was generally over-estimated since financial innovation was mitigating the disintermediation effects of higher interest rates through which monetary policy had traditionally operated;

- The fall of the dollar from September 1977 onward might also have been taken as evidence that policy was too expansionary. But in its early stages this fall was seen as a useful corrective of an over-valued dollar that was contributing to the growing current-account deficit. Indeed, for much of 1978, when dollar depreciation was being viewed with increasing alarm within the Administration, it tended to be interpreted primarily as a market response to the current-account deficit. Although some officials were already warning that rising inflation expectations were a growing factor in the dollar's decline, this view was not generally supported within the Administration. In this context, the Administration responded by actions to curtail oil imports and such "bridging" actions as Treasury gold sales, rather than by tightening policy. Indeed, as late as the Bonn Summit in July 1978, the principal action being pressed on the United States by the other countries was to curtail its oil demand as its contribution to concerted action. External adjustment, rather than inflation, may thus still have been perceived as the overriding issue, even though the current-account deficit had in fact begun to decline.

If there was no totally unambiguous flashing alarm – other, perhaps, than inflation itself – it is clear that, at least from the beginning of 1978, concern about inflation began to percolate through the Administration, albeit in an uneven way, with different agencies of government reassessing their views at different times. As a result, the Administration remained divided both on the severity of the inflation problem and on how to deal with it for much of the year, and market perceptions that the Administration was ambivalent, and unwilling to take policy decisions at variance with its basic views about the inflation/unemployment trade-off, was a factor that probably contributed to the renewed decline of the dollar from August onward.

The fall of the dollar, in turn, played an important, though as it turned out not decisive, role in catalysing concern about inflation. While, as noted above, it was not generally agreed that the falling dollar was itself an indicator of excessively expansionary policy, it was clearly recognised that the dollar fall could cause inflation to rise. Stabilizing the dollar became an Administration priority in 1978 in large part because depreciation was threatening to undermine the wage-price guidelines that constituted the key operational element of the Administration's anti-inflation policy. It is also clear that the timing, as well as the thrust of the October 1979 policy change by the Fed was heavily influenced by the renewed fall of the dollar (and the increasingly vocal "peer pressure" on the Chairman and other U.S. officials from other central bankers and finance ministers). The fall of the dollar, finally, gave rise within the Administration to a more pessimistic view about the medium-term prospects for the dollar as the key currency of the international monetary system. The concern that the dollar would remain under downward pressure for an extended period because of the assumed transition to a multi-currency reserve system motivated the initially favourable U.S. reaction to the idea of a Substitution Account within the IMF as an instrument for eliminating the perceived "dollar overhang" in an orderly way.

Assessment

With hindsight, the overall picture of this episode is one in which expansionary policies were pursued for too long, resulting in an acceleration of inflation to politically intolerable levels, which in turn necessitated a decisive shift to restrictive monetary policy and subsequent recession. In this perspective, it is the shift in October 1979 in the Federal Reserve's operating procedures that constitute the key "turning point" in policy. (Perhaps, somewhat more broadly, it was the appointment of Paul Volcker as Chairman of the Fed that should be regarded as the decisive event since it was the policy intent of the Federal Reserve and the Administration, rather than the operating procedures as such, that really mattered in the subsequent attack on inflation.) Thus, the dollar-stabilization actions of November 1978, though an important stepping stone in the story (and, in terms of market perceptions, a big success) appear more as a palliative response to a crisis situation than a fundamental change of course.

The year 1978 stands out as the year of "missed opportunity". At least by mid-year, sufficient evidence that a change of course was needed had become available. But the Administration proved unable to organise an effective response. There was perhaps an excessive element of fine-tuning in the actions that were taken: interest rate hikes were frequent, but generally came later than the market expected and were already discounted as inadequate when announced. Other policy actions gave out mixed signals: the administrative machinery of wage-price standards was strengthened, but at the same time an expansionary tax cut was signed into law. This approach worked badly both because it confused markets and because it tended to give policy makers the impression that action was being taken, when in fact little was being achieved.

By the beginning of 1979 the need to focus on the inflation problem as the top priority for economic policy was recognised almost universally within the Administration. But translating this concern into effective action was, in the end, dependent on bringing "new players" into the policy arena. Adjustments to the existing approach were possible (a tighter budget for FY 1980, a strengthening of the wage-price standards etc.) and (in the absence of the second oil shock) might have produced some positive results. But to "get out in front" of the inflation process required, in the end, a change in assumptions about the nature of the inflation/output trade-off and the relevant time-horizon for making policy. Unlike the foreign exchange crisis of 1978, which reached a well-defined climax where decisive action could not be deferred, the inflation problem continued to build in a corrosive and unsustainable way, but without producing any single event which would galvanise the political will to take decisive action. This mobilisation of political will may have been essentially dependent on having on hand a new way of thinking about policy. President Carter's appointment of Mr. Volcker to the Fed with a mandate to fight inflation was the first step here. The support by the new Administration that came to power in 1981 for rigorously disinflationary monetary policy was the essential follow-up.

Chapter 3

Japan, 1976-79:
riding the roller-coaster

Introduction

This chapter is concerned with economic and policy developments in Japan during the 1976-79 period. In summary, this period was marked on the external side by the emergence of a large current-account surplus and a strong appreciation of the yen (to some extent the counterpart of accelerating dollar weakness) and on the domestic side by demand growth that was weak relative to historical experience and then-current estimates of potential. In response to these developments monetary policy was eased progressively and fiscal policy was set on a very expansionary course in 1977-78. While these actions contributed to stronger growth of domestic demand they also imposed substantial costs by leaving a legacy of large government debt and reduced fiscal flexibility. Under the combined impact of expansionary policy and yen appreciation, the current account surplus turned into deficit in 1979, and the yen in turn weakened so that by March 1980 most of the 1977-78 appreciation had been reversed.

This episode needs to be placed in the longer-run context of the evolution of the Japanese economy. Until near the end of the 1960s Japan had tended to be a deficit country facing a balance-of-payments constraint; but then in the early 1970s Japan went into large surplus and encountered increasing trade friction (with the United States in particular). The "Nixon shock" and the sharp appreciation of the yen following the breakdown of the Bretton Woods' System faced the Japanese economy with problems in many respects analogous to those that arose in the period being reviewed in this note. But the process of adjustment to the high yen that got underway in 1972-73 was interrupted by the first oil-price shock which was particularly traumatic for Japan because of its high dependence on imported energy. The terms-of-trade loss pushed Japan back into large external deficit, and the yen weakened, thereby accelerating the trade-volume adjustments that were needed to pay for expensive oil. The more-rapid-than-expected adjustment of the Japanese economy to these new circumstances to some extent set the stage for the episode under consideration.

A second aspect of longer-term Japanese economic performance that is important for this episode is the very rapid decline in the growth of Japanese potential output from the early 1970s onward. While technical studies prior to the period under consideration had already documented that such a slowdown was taking place, and of course the oil-price shock had also traumatised expectations, it remained extremely difficult to assess the growth of potential output in the period following the oil price shock. Assessments inside the Japanese government diverged on this issue, with the Economic Planning Agency's estimate of 5.7 per cent perhaps representing a central view. International organisations retained substantially higher estimates. With hindsight, even the EPA estimate was probably over-optimistic.

The episode also needs to be seen in a broader international context. The period was one in which high growth was very much an international priority, as reflected for example in the "Strategy for Sustained Economic Expansion" adopted at the OECD Ministerial meeting in June 1976, the "McCracken Report" issued in June of 1977, and more generally the locomotive theory that evolved out of the work of the Trilateral Commission. As regards financial developments, the international context also needs to be kept in mind. Although yen appreciation during this period was in part the reaction of markets to the Japanese current-account surplus, the exchange-rate "crisis" of 1978 was not a yen crisis but a dollar crisis: loss of confidence in the dollar had its counterpart, more or less simultaneously though in varying degrees, in the appreciation of all major non-dollar currencies. The economic policies of all countries were, to some extent, matters for international negotiation. Thus, for example, international pressure on Japan to take actions to reduce its current-account surplus was countered by Japanese urgings to the U.S. authorities to tighten their monetary policy, cut oil imports, or otherwise increase the competitiveness of American producers. Yet the international economic diplomacy of Japan in this period was not simply a matter of negotiating concessions. Japan was keen, as a major economic player on the world scene to demonstrate its willingness to take a greater share of responsibility for the proper functioning of the world economy. Japan's growth-oriented posture at the 1977 London Summit, and the Japanese commitment to 7 per cent growth in fiscal year 1978 which was formalised at the Bonn Summit needs to be seen, at least in part, as an expression of this view of Japan's global responsibility.

The episode

The recovery from the 1974-75 recession got underway in mid-1975, with exports providing the main initial source of strength. The foundations for this had been laid by the depreciation of the yen in the wake of the oil shock which left Japan in a strong competitive position at the start of the global recovery: export volumes (customs basis) grew by over 20 per cent in 1976. At the same time, the beginnings of the restructuring of Japanese industry away from raw materials-intensive products, together with a protracted phase of de-stocking, meant that import growth remained relatively subdued in relation to industrial production. As a result of these developments, and roughly stable terms of trade, the current-account deficit with which Japan began this period had turned into surplus by the end of 1976.

In the course of 1976, domestic demand also started to recover, as a result of monetary relaxation which began in April 1975 and the subsequent adoption of expansionary fiscal policy later in the same year. But domestic demand growth in 1976 (at 4.7 per cent) was still modest compared to Japanese experience before the oil shock and then-current estimates of potential. Relatively healthy GNP growth (6.5 per cent as measured at the then-used 1970 price base) was thus of a markedly export-led character.

Some problems began to appear in 1977. International discussions on the medium-term economic strategy and balance of payments adjustment had often viewed an average annual growth rate of around 7 per cent for Japan as desirable in view of Japan's GNP potential, and initial official Japanese projections for 1977 were in line with this view: GNP was projected to grow at 6.7 per cent, with a growing contribution from domestic demand, and only a moderate current-account surplus. Such projections were judged to be consistent with the policy stance, since fiscal policy was maintained on an expansionary course for FY 1977, including a sharp 20 per cent increase in public works expenditure. Domestic demand, however, proved weaker than the authorities had expected. While export growth began to slow in volume terms, imports also decelerated sharply and the current-account surplus continued to widen under the impact of strengthening terms of trade. Partly in response to this, the yen (which had already appreciated some 5 per cent in effective terms in 1976) began to appreciate strongly, and by mid-1977 had returned to pre-oil-shock levels.

As evidence of weaker-than-expected domestic demand became available, a new series of expansionary measures were adopted. The discount rate, which had remained unchanged in 1976 was lowered three times during the course of 1977 (to 4.25 per cent in September) for a cumulative decline of 4.75 percentage points from the 9 per cent rate that had prevailed from late 1973 to early 1975. This course was also justified because inflation, particularly at the wholesale price level, was decelerating sharply under the influence of yen appreciation. A supplementary budget was proposed in October, further increasing public works expenditures, and yet another supplementary budget was announced in December. In this process, the 30 per cent norm for the deficit/expenditure ratio that had been laid down in 1976 was breached.

By late 1977, the economic situation and policy choices facing the Japanese authorities had become very complex. While leading indicators of Japanese exports available to the authorities were already pointing to a noticeable weakening, the current-account surplus in nominal terms was still growing, and was becoming the lightning-rod for increasing trade friction with other countries. Further yen appreciation was increasingly unpalatable, but exchange-market intervention proved to have limited effects in the face of strong market expectations for further appreciation. Measures to limit capital inflows that were introduced in November 1977 and extended in March 1978 likewise proved to have only limited and temporary effects. Both domestically and internationally there was strong pressure on the Japanese government to achieve faster growth as a way to moderate the current-account surplus, but strong growth was becoming more difficult to achieve because, in volume terms, the contribution of net exports to GNP growth had already turned negative, and yen appreciation was undermining business confidence and investment. Further fiscal action thus appeared necessary if strong growth was to be achieved, but deficit financing had already exceeded the limits of what the financial authorities considered at all sustainable.

Amid these conflicting considerations, the Japanese government adopted a forecast of 7 per cent growth for FY 1978 and proposed yet another expansionary budget in order to achieve this. (The initial FY 1978 budget, together with the supplementary budget announced in December 1977 comprised what was called the "15 month budget".) In the face of further yen appreciation, monetary policy was also eased further, with a cut in the discount rate in March 1978 to the then unprecedented low level of 3 1/2 per cent. This was the first time in five years that external considerations were explicitly mentioned in the announcement of a monetary policy action.

While the 7 per cent forecast was not a target, it did have a strong normative element. During the course of 1978, the distinction between forecast and target became further eroded, as international "recommendations" and their repercussions in the Japanese press gave this number increasing weight. Progressively, 7 per cent came to be viewed, both domestically and internationally, as a target that the

Japanese government was committed to achieving. This was formalised at the Bonn Summit in July 1978 when Japan officially adopted this target as its contribution to concerted action.

Domestic demand had already begun to recover strongly in the fourth quarter of 1977, and accelerated further during the first half of 1978 (to almost 10 per cent annual rate in the second quarter). But net exports in volume terms were becoming powerfully negative even as the current account surplus, driven by J-curve effects, rose to a peak of almost $ 19 billion (annual rate) in the first quarter and remained on a high plateau for the next two. As a result, it became clear by late Summer 1978 that the GNP growth target would not be reached without further action. A large package of economic measures amounting to about 1.3 per cent of GNP was thus announced in September, and a supplementary budget for implementing these measures was approved by the Diet in October.

Even this action, which was generally recognised internationally as a full implementation of Japan's summit commitment, did not in the end produce the 7 per cent growth of GNP – though by the time this became apparent Japan's current-account surplus had disappeared and with it the international attention on Japanese growth.

If, during 1978, the international political focus was on growth, the essential economic management problem for Japan was to live through the relentless upward pressure on the yen until 1st November, when the United States finally took stabilization actions on the dollar. From end-1976 to November 1978, the yen had appreciated by about 60 per cent against the dollar, and 46 per cent on an effective basis. Despite Japanese efforts to enlist the United States in co-ordinated actions to stem currency movements, no effective internationally co-ordinated approach was put in place. In its absence, there was little that the Japanese government could effectively do to stem the rise of the yen. Neither monetary policy nor capital control measures nor at times massive intervention had much effect in the face of market perceptions that Japan's current-account surplus was unsustainable and, perhaps as important, the growing loss of confidence in the dollar and resulting portfolio diversification. To the extent that yen appreciation was being driven by the current account surplus, but J-curve effects from appreciation were simultaneously preventing the surplus from coming down, this constituted a sort of vicious circle whose effect was to prolong the period of yen appreciation and drive it to unrealistic heights. Bringing the surplus down was thus a key priority of the Japanese government. The ambitious growth target was one means to achieve this; but the government also took direct actions in the Summer of 1978 to try to restrain exports and promote imports – notably through the Emergency Import Program.

These direct actions may have contributed to the decline of the current-account surplus in the fourth quarter of 1978, but by then the fundamental situation was changing dramatically. With the dollar stabilization measures of 1st November, the yen turned around so that, with J-curves operating in reverse, the underlying trade-volume adjustments of the last year were compounded by adverse price movements, with the result that the current-account moved into deficit with surprising speed in the first quarter of 1979.

The growth momentum that had been built up through two years of expansionary policies carried over into 1979, despite the disruptive effects of the second oil-price shock; GNP grew by 5.6 per cent (about the same as in 1978). Although the government, in presenting the FY 1979 budget, had aimed for a somewhat less expansionary stance (notably through a slowdown in the rate of increase of public works investment from 27 per cent in FY 1978 to 20 per cent in FY 1979), the deficit ratio widened further under the impact of large declines in corporate tax revenue. (This was perhaps the first indication of how difficult it would prove to be to reverse fiscal course − a problem that became a matter of increasing preoccupation for the Japanese government after 1980.)

Financial developments during 1979 were in many respects the mirror image of 1978. While the initial depreciation of the yen in late 1978 had been welcomed, this soon became a preoccupation as the decline showed no signs of ending, and inflation began to rise. The rise in import prices associated with yen depreciation was exacerbated by the rise in oil prices which also intensified pressure on the yen since markets saw higher oil prices as "bad for Japan". In April 1979 the discount rate was raised, and two further increases occurred later in the year. Intervention by the Japanese authorities to support the yen began on a massive scale in March (during March/April Japanese reserves fell by $ 6.6 billion), and controls on capital inflows that had been established in 1977-78 were abolished. While domestic inflation concerns warranted the direction of monetary policy toward restraint, so that there was no conflict between internal and external objectives, the absence of international willingness to engage in co-ordinated actions to forestall the re-emergence of an undervalued yen may have left the Japanese authorities with little choice in the matter. Yen depreciation continued, despite the efforts by the Japanese government to counter it, through to the first quarter of 1980, by which time about four-fifths of the effective appreciation of the preceding two years had been reversed. It was brought to an end, finally, after a joint announcement of major central banks on 2nd March, 1980 that actions to support the yen would be taken and a dramatic 1.75 percentage point rise in the Japanese discount rate to a "crisis" level of 9 per cent announced somewhat later in the same month.

Main policy considerations

The broad thrust of policy during this period can readily be interpreted as a coherent response to the prevailing economic conditions. Fiscal and monetary policy were broadly consistent with the policy paradigm that was then dominant in Japan (and most other OECD countries), which stressed activist use of fiscal policy for demand management. Furthermore, given the then prevailing views about potential, the emerging current-account surplus could easily be seen as at least in large part a cyclical phenomenon that would disappear as actual GNP was brought up to potential. Structural considerations were not, at that time, given due attention. At the same time, inflation, though still high at the start of the period, began to come down during 1977 so that more relaxed monetary policy could be judged appropriate on domestic grounds. Finally, as regards the exchange rate, traditional instruments of intervention (and a still-substantial degree of control over capital movements) were used to moderate its movements (with perhaps less-than-hoped-for success); but the Japanese authorities had broadly accepted the notion that exchange-rate determination should basically be left to the market. The appreciation of the yen was, at least in its earlier phases, consistent with fundamentals and – in any event – not necessarily controllable by the Japanese authorities in the absence of U.S. action on the dollar.

What is thus striking about this period is not the qualitative pattern of policy actions, but their intensity – in particular the extreme degree of fiscal expansion that was implemented in 1978. A number of factors were influential in this decision, and it is difficult to disentangle their relative importance. The principal consideration might be summarised as follows:

a) *The current-account surplus.* Memories of the period leading up to the "Nixon shock" were still very much alive, and in particular the threat of protectionist actions abroad if the surplus should grow too large. In the early 1970s, a limit to the surplus at 1 per cent of GNP had been incorporated in Japanese planning. While no precise targets for the current-account existed during the period being considered in this note, large surpluses were broadly viewed by the authorities as *politically* unsustainable because of the risk of trade conflicts. Indeed, rising trade friction during 1977 and into 1978 (voluntary export restraints on televisions, the trigger-price system on steel) gave point to these concerns;

b) *Domestic pressures.* There were important domestic constituencies pushing for stronger growth, particularly among those business sectors – such as steel – who were being subjected to administrative export restraints. In part, these pressures may have reflected the view that (as with the "income

41

doubling plan" of the 1960s) expansionary policies would prove to be self-validating. More immediately, concern that yen appreciation would squeeze profits on exports and limit further export growth may have made domestic expansion seem desirable as a way of reducing the current-account surplus and taking pressure off the yen;

c) *International pressures.* Direct "peer pressure" on Japanese authorities to pursue more expansionary policies played a major role. Indeed, at the highest level of government, a strong growth objective for Japan was viewed as an appropriate contribution to improved global economic performance (the locomotive theory). Supporters of this view within the Administration may have particularly welcomed foreign "peer pressure" as an instrument for winning over their less-enthusiastic colleagues;

d) *The growth target.* A striking feature of the episode was the extent to which the domestic and international policy debate centred on the adoption of a specific number for economic growth. Perhaps the success of Japan during the 1960s in achieving or exceeding planned objectives obscured to some extent the risks associated with staking policy to the achievement of a growth objective – namely that, since growth as such is not directly controll-able and to some extent a hostage to exogenous developments, the policy consequences of such an objective are unpredictable and perhaps extreme. Be that as it may, it seems clear that the supplementary budgets of 1977, and especially the September 1978 supplementary budget were direct consequences of the international commitments that Japan had made to achieving its stated growth target.

As regards the choice of policy instruments, priority was given to fiscal expansion, through public works investment in particular, largely because – given the high savings rate of Japanese households – such action was judged more effective than tax cuts in promoting demand growth. In addition (and in sharp contrast to other countries) the Japanese government was able to implement public works spending decision very rapidly – and indeed to control the flow of such spending in a very flexible manner – so that this instrument appeared attractive for demand management. Also, at this time (and in contrast to 1986-87), sectors of the economy which had been hardest hit by yen appreciation, such as steel, could benefit directly from public works. Yet already at the time (and of course with much greater force subsequently) doubts about the efficacy, inherent limitations, and (most importantly perhaps) debt consequences of fiscal action were also being expressed.

42

Assessment

With hindsight, it is clear that the efficacy of fiscal expansion in bringing about strong output growth was over-estimated – in turn perhaps a reflection of the fact that supply-side constraints on the feasible rate of expansion were under-estimated. Indeed, as noted at various points above, the over-estimation of potential output may have been at the core of the problem.

It is difficult to assess the role that policy played in bringing about external adjustment. The direct contribution of fiscal expansion to domestic demand growth, and so to higher imports, was one element in the adjustment, but it seems clear that the appreciation of the yen was by far more decisive. Economic theory would suggest that fiscal expansion, operating against a background of stable growth of the monetary aggregates (as was the case during this period) might have contributed indirectly to external adjustment by promoting yen appreciation. But, on balance, yen appreciation during this period appeared more closely linked to the current-account surplus in nominal terms than to real interest-rate differentials as would be predicted by this model.

Again with hindsight, it also seems clear that the longer-term costs of fiscal expansion were under-estimated. In the end, it came to be the rising share of government debt that was considered the unsustainable element of Japanese policy. Beginning in 1980, fiscal retrenchment became the dominant priority, although some use of fiscal policy for demand management continued within the medium-term framework of fiscal consolidation.

Another problematic aspect of the episode – though one that was far from controllable by the Japanese authorities themselves – was the overshooting of the exchange rate on the upside in 1978, and on the downside in 1979, with consequent large oscillations in the current account. The reluctance of the U.S. Administration during much of 1978 to take stronger action to limit dollar overshooting, as well as the European move in 1978 to establish the European Monetary System (which became effective in March 1979) as a means of limiting fluctuations in the effective exchange rates of their currencies left the yen vulnerable to larger fluctuations both against the dollar and in effective terms. Whether, in this context, and in the absence of stronger international commitments to exchange-rate stability, more could or should have been done by the Japanese authorities themselves is uncertain. Monetary policy, in particular, was to some extent constrained in the timing of its actions by the need to preserve reasonable relationships among different interest rates – many of which were still administered and adjustable only with a considerable negotiating lag.

Other instruments were extensively used, and if results were disappointing this has to be attributed to the inherent limitations of these instruments.

One lesson that was drawn from this experience is the limited effectiveness of capital controls as an instrument for managing the exchange rate. Japan's international transactions had simply become too large for this approach to remain feasible or indeed desirable. In 1980 a new law governing foreign exchange transactions was implemented, based on the rule that such transactions were "free in principle".

Another lesson that was clearly illustrated by this episode is the very substantial divergence that can arise between the movement of the external accounts in *volume* terms and in value terms when it is the exchange rate that is driving the adjustment process. To the extent that market attention focuses on value data, the exchange rate is subject to overshooting – a problem which may not have any easy solution.

A final point of assessment suggested by this episode is the extreme care that needs to be used in relying on normative forecasts in the setting of policy. Not only can such forecasts become stumbling blocks to policy if the underlying assumptions prove wrong, or if unexpected shocks intervene; but they can also become stumbling blocks to effective international discussion. To the extent that the political commitment to such normative forecasts makes them extremely difficult to change, even when incoming data suggests that they are unrealistic, there is a risk that credibility is impaired.

Chapter 4

Germany, 1977-82:
from demand management to consolidation

Introduction

This chapter focuses on two periods of considerable policy interest for Germany: the period of strong upward pressure on the DM in 1977-78 which was largely the counterpart of the loss of confidence in the dollar; and the 1980-81 period of external deficit and a weakening currency, which culminated in the "shock therapy" administered in February 1981.

By 1977-78 economic policy in Germany had already begun to be formulated in a medium-term context. This was especially the case for monetary policy for which the transition to a regime of floating exchange rates in 1973 was seen as a watershed. The Bundesbank was now considered able to pursue an effective policy of monetary control, oriented primarily towards domestic goals – ultimately price stability and economic growth. Beginning with the year 1975, monetary policy was framed in terms of monetary targets – more specifically, annual targets for the growth of central bank money. The exchange rate of the DM was allowed to move fairly freely in response to changes in economic "fundamentals" to insulate the domestic economy from external shocks, and notably the German price level from world inflation. Intervention was to consist mainly of short-term smoothing operations: European monetary arrangements allowed fairly frequent parity realignments, and domestic monetary repercussions were to be taken into consideration in deciding the size of purchases and sales of foreign exchange outside these arrangements.

As a result of a variety of forces, including a changing perception of domestic problems and needs, fiscal policy was in the early stages of a major reassessment and reorientation at the time of the first episode. Among certain policy makers, a shift of emphasis from demand-side to supply-side considerations, and from the short term to the medium term, had already begun. A decade or more of reliance on demand-side policies seemed responsible for growing rigidities and bottlenecks in the economy, making full employment less compatible with price stability and carrying the threat of more sluggish growth. Because of expectations that the authorities would *de facto* assure a high level of real demand, the wage-setting process tended to yield excessive increases in nominal wages; there was concern that profits would be progressively undermined, leading to sub-optimum investment in the economy. A proliferation of microeconomic measures – such as subsidies and grants, social protection for workers, and labour dismissal compensations – raised fears that, even though each one of these measures seemed justified and probably had little or no adverse side-effects, in aggregate they might result in a serious reduction of labour mobility and create disincentives to carrying out the necessary lay-offs and restructuring.

But despite these considerations and growing worries about the longer-term sustainability of budget deficits, the main concern of fiscal policy throughout these two episodes remained to support real demand and promote growth, either through tax cuts or increased government spending. This reflected not only inertia and the difficulty of reaching agreement on specific aspects of a major reorientation of fiscal policy but also the very special conditions of the 1970s – a decade marked by the two oil shocks and a high degree of uncertainty in economic affairs. As a result, government expenditure as a percentage of GNP, after increasing rapidly in the early 1970s and reaching some 50 per cent in 1975, fluctuated around that level for several years and it was not until 1982 that it began to decline. The budget deficit as a percentage of GNP reached a peak of some 6 per cent in 1975, and in 1982 was still at around 4 per cent.

The episode: 1977-78

Following the recession of 1975, the German economy had a rapid recovery from mid-1975 until mid-1976 but thereafter its growth performance became less satisfactory. While inflation was reduced significantly, unemployment remained historically high (around 4 per cent). Despite the appreciation of the DM, in real as well as in nominal terms, the current account remained in surplus (although it was less than 1 per cent of GDP, compared to 2.7 in 1974). In the course of 1977, the emphasis of fiscal policy was progressively shifted from budget consolidation towards supporting demand. Monetary policy also became more expansionary and interest rates declined. The rise of domestic demand and output accelerated markedly in the course of 1978 and unemployment fell somewhat (to 3.7 per cent for the year as a whole). Nonetheless, the external surplus widened.

46

In 1976-77, net outflows of long-term capital had been an important offset of the current account surplus: the appreciation of the exchange rate and the increase in net external reserves basically reflected inflows of short-term funds – monetary and non-monetary. But in 1978, expectations of a further appreciation of the DM led to a sharp reduction of long-term outflows and stepped-up inflows of short-term monetary funds. This upward pressure on the DM was, to a large extent, the mirror image of the weakness of the dollar: hence, it was motivated as much by disappointment and scepticism with respect to the dollar and the U.S. economy as by confidence in the DM and the performance of the German economy – notably in terms of inflation and foreign trade. In this context, the role of the DM as a reserve currency increased. Funds were shifted on a large scale from dollar assets to a small number of strong currencies of which the DM was perhaps the most important. To contain the appreciation of the DM, the Bundesbank intervened substantially in the first quarter of 1978. In March, the Bundesbank and the Federal Reserve System agreed to double their reciprocal swap lines to $ 4 billion. The U.S. Treasury announced the sale of SDR 600 million to the Bundesbank to acquire DM, and mentioned the possibility of IMF drawings by the United States. After a lull of a few months, strong upward pressure on the DM resumed in the summer and the German authorities intervened in a massive way. Finally, on 1st November, with conditions in foreign exchange markets approaching crisis level, the U.S. authorities adopted a comprehensive dollar support programme. The dollar rebounded somewhat and the DM, in effective terms, levelled off. Nonetheless, the Bundesbank continued to intervene in co-ordination not only with other major European countries and Japan but now also with the United States.

For 1978 as a whole, the increase in German net official reserves amounted to an unprecedented $ 10 billion – marginally more than the previous record of 1973. The current-account surplus increased to $ 9 billion or 1.4 per cent of GDP, and net outflows of long-term capital dropped to less than $ 1½ billion. Net inflow of short-term monetary funds reached some $ 5 billion but, somewhat surprisingly, short-term non-monetary transactions recorded a small outflow. The appreciation of the DM, in terms of the OECD effective exchange-rate index, was limited to 4 per cent in 1978: but this brought the cumulative appreciation since end-1975 to 25 per cent. In real terms, the appreciation of the DM from end-1975 to end-1978 was some 7 per cent on the basis of consumer prices but 16 per cent on the basis of unit labour costs. The intervention carried out by the Bundesbank and the policy of low interest rates led to a significant overshooting of the target for central bank money (11.4 per cent compared to a target of 8 per cent). Moreover, in fulfilment of Germany's pledge at the July Bonn Summit, the government adopted a fiscal programme to strengthen demand and improve growth which contained net tax reductions and additional public spending totalling some DM 12 billion or 1 per cent of GDP.

1980-81

Partly as a result of the fiscal measures taken in 1978, the German economy was on a strong upswing and had a head start in the international trade cycle when it was hit by the second oil shock in 1979. That year, real GDP grew at more than 4 per cent and the rate of unemployment decreased to 3.2 per cent, the lowest level since 1974. But reflecting domestic factors, including large increases in wages and labour costs, inflationary tensions were growing and this trend was accentuated by the rise in oil and other commodity prices. The current account recorded a massive deterioration of some $ 15 billion or 2 per cent of GDP, and moved into a deficit of $ 6 billion – the first deficit since 1965. In early 1980, fiscal policy became less expansionary and monetary policy was progressively tightened: the discount rate was increased twice and administrative measures affecting capital inflows were relaxed. Combined with the contractionary impact of the oil shock and the deterioration of the current account in volume terms, the different stance of economic policy resulted in a pronounced reduction of real growth in the second half of the year. Unemployment rose again, but inflation continued to increase as the effect of higher oil prices was accentuated by a progressive depreciation of the DM. For 1980 as a whole, the current account deficit widened to nearly $ 16 billion or 2 per cent of GDP. To help its financing the authorities borrowed substantial amounts (in DM) directly from official institutions of a few OPEC countries. This form of "compensatory financing" resulted in official long-term capital inflows of some $ 12 billion in 1980, an amount practically equivalent to that of all private capital outflows. Hence, the current account deficit was fully reflected in a deterioration of net official reserves. Gross reserves decreased by some $ 6½ billion to $ 48½ billion (excluding gold), and Bundesbank liabilities towards foreign monetary authorities increased by nearly $ 9 billion, largely as a result of intervention to support the DM within the EMS.

In view of the weakness of the economy, the stance of monetary policy was eased somewhat in the second half of 1980, and the Lombard rate was lowered by ½ point to 9 per cent in September. This widened the unfavourable interest differential with the United States, where the discount rate had recently been raised to 11 per cent. Perhaps also reflecting the political crisis in Poland, sentiment in foreign exchange markets turned strongly against the DM. Large capital outflows took place in the last months of 1980 and the Bundesbank intervened heavily to support the DM. These interventions, which were largely sterilised, proved ineffective in offsetting exchange-rate pressure and a crisis of confidence emerged in early 1981. In February 1981, the Bundesbank responded by taking a series of exceptional measures – including closing the normal Lombard window and activating the special Lombard facility – which resulted in a steep rise in interest rates and provided a powerful signalling effect[1].

48

These measures were followed by a sharp turnaround in private capital flows and the Bundesbank regained reserves as a result of intervention *vis-à-vis* some EMS currencies. The DM remained weak against the dollar but moved to the top of the EMS band and in October 1981 was revalued (by 5.5 per cent) against other Member currencies. This caused a reflow of funds out of Germany so that for 1981 as a whole, private capital movements were still negative. But as compensatory financing was again very large, official capital recorded a net inflow of $ 7½ billion. The current-account deficit was reduced to $ 5 billion and net official reserves fell only slightly. The period of slow or negative growth, which had started in 1980, continued in 1981-82. The current account moved into surplus again in 1982 but, despite the strong improvement of German competitiveness, especially in terms of unit labour costs, the surplus remained modest. With high interest rates in the United States and a strong dollar, German monetary policy was relaxed step by step beginning in the Autumn of 1982, but interest rates remained historically high, in nominal as well as in real terms. As for fiscal policy, in the context of rising budget deficits and a growing share of government in the economy, the phase of 1975-82 – which had sought to stimulate domestic demand – was, starting in 1982, succeeded by a long period of fiscal consolidation.

Main policy considerations: 1977-78

This episode of exchange-rate pressure was perceived by the German authorities as being essentially of foreign origin – the strength of the DM being largely the mirror image of the weakness of the dollar and the loss of confidence in U.S. economic policy. The situation was nonetheless somewhat paradoxical; Germany was running a large and persistent budget deficit; domestic inflation was still around 4 per cent, reflecting the pressure of wages and labour costs; and the money supply was overshooting as the combined result of the financing of the budget deficit by the banking system, the rapid expansion of domestic credit, and official intervention in the exchange market. And yet, the current-account surplus was growing and the currency was under upward pressure. Given this context, the prevailing view among the authorities was that a fairly large appreciation of the DM could be tolerated since in addition to promoting external adjustment, it would put downward pressure on wages, costs and prices and therefore limit inflation. Hence, in the first part of the episode there seemed to be little or no dilemma. The exchange rate was largely allowed to take the brunt, and official market intervention continued to be essentially for smoothing purposes. The overshooting of the money supply was seen as a temporary departure from longer-term norms, justified by the initial slack in the economy, the external surplus and the contribution to price stability expected from the appreciation of the currency; but the authorities were from the very beginning aware of the fact that the massive liquidity build-up in the economy could entail an inflation danger once appreciation pressures abated. Fiscal policy was mainly aiming at supporting domestic demand and promoting internal growth, an objective consistent with the desire to see the current-account surplus reduced to a more normal level. According to the German authorities, this notion of a "normal" current-account level cannot be given a precise definition or quantification, as it tends to vary according to the international context as well as domestic conditions and policies. Nonetheless, they feel that it is a useful concept and that, as a broad generalisation, a small surplus on the current account can probably be regarded as normal or appropriate to support inter alia the capital outflows to developing countries that a mature economy, like Germany, is expected to generate.

While the continuing appreciation of the DM since early 1976 did not seem to pose insurmountable problems to German exporters, it was nonetheless feared that the erosion of international competitiveness and the related profit squeeze could jeopardise the recovery in fixed investment which had just begun after a protracted period of weakness. In the course of 1978 it also became increasingly evident that to allow the exchange rate to rise sufficiently to absorb the excess demand for DM stemming from diversification of international portfolios could seriously undermine some of the macroeconomic objectives of monetary policy. A lasting overvaluation of the currency would not only threaten the exposed sectors of the economy but also provide wrong price signals to economic agents and lead to a misallocation of resources. On the other hand, the authorities were reluctant to accommodate the excess demand for DM through the creation of additional liquidity because of its potentially adverse impact on price stability and because it would have allowed the internationalisation of the DM to proceed at an excessively fast pace. The authorities were prepared to accept a reserve currency role for the DM, but did not wish actively to promote it. Given the magnitudes involved, sterilised intervention seemed incapable of solving this dilemma, and owing to the deep-seated commitment of the German authorities to a system of free capital movements, except for a few selective measures to discourage capital inflows, systematic exchange controls were never seriously considered.

In the event, during the crisis period of 1978, the Bundesbank opted for a policy of large, unsterilised intervention, and accepted the over-shooting of its monetary targets. This response to the dilemma between adhering to the monetary aggregate target or maintaining a broadly unchanged exchange rate was essentially dictated by the expected repercussions on the ultimate domestic goals of economic policy, namely price stability and real growth. While for the reasons just mentioned, a major further

50

appreciation of the exchange rate was considered a serious threat to economic growth, the overshooting of the money supply did not seem to pose an immediate danger to prices and wages: it was hoped that exchange-rate pressure would abate or reverse itself, and that the excessive liquidity could be reabsorbed before it would significantly affect the rate of inflation. There were uncertainties about the margin of slack in the economy, but on balance it was believed to be still significant and to justify further measures in support of demand. According to official figures of that time, utilisation of productive capacity was still below 95 per cent in 1978, compared to a level of "normal utilisation" put at around 97 per cent. The fiscal package introduced after the Bonn Summit was in line with this view. Hence, with respect to fiscal policy there appeared to be no serious conflict between internal and external requirements during this episode. It is with respect to monetary policy that a conflict can be said to have emerged in 1978, and policy actions were primarily designed to keep the German economy on course in the face of disequilibria generated abroad.

1980-81

The proximate cause of the weakening of the DM in foreign exchange markets in 1980 was the rapid and massive deterioration of the current account as a result of the strong upswing of the German economy ahead of its major trading partners in 1979, the important cumulative appreciation of the DM in real terms over the previous years, and the new sharp increase in oil prices. At first, the authorities seemed to regard the external deficit as relatively tolerable, perhaps because to a significant extent it reflected the second oil shock, and it could be argued that, owing to their special character, "oil deficits" still had to be partly accepted (i.e. financed) until structural changes and longer-term corrective measures would reabsorb them. Hence, the German authorities relied heavily on a special form of compensatory financing, that is direct borrowing in domestic currency from official institutions of a few OPEC countries. With the economy moving into a phase of slow or negative growth, a tightening of monetary policy in the first half of 1980 was partially reversed in the second half, even though interest rates were rising in the United States and the dollar was strengthening. Given the deflationary impact of the second oil shock on domestic demand and the reduction of net exports, fiscal policy remained supportive of demand.

Thus, until late in the episode, the monetary authorities tried, through compensatory financing and sterilised intervention, to circumvent the growing dilemma between internal and external requirements. But a conflict was also clearly developing between the ultimate domestic objectives of price stability and economic growth.

Relative priority was given to supporting domestic demand and employment, perhaps because it was felt that the acceleration of inflation resulting from the increase in oil prices would be essentially a short-lived affair, unlikely to become embedded in the economy given the important margin of slack. But the relaxation of monetary policy in the second half of 1980 in the face of an unsatisfactory cost-price performance and a tightening of monetary conditions in the United States apparently raised doubts about the anti-inflationary resolve of the authorities, and the foreign exchange market reacted negatively. Persistent weakness of the DM raised the spectre of a depreciation-induced inflationary spiral. Such concerns were magnified by the position of the DM as a second-line reserve currency, which the German authorities feel puts the DM in an especially vulnerable and asymmetrical position. This is because it is felt that funds will flow in when the dominant reserve currency is in trouble and will flow out again as soon as the dominant reserve currency recovers – and all this regardless of the economic performance of Germany. Moreover, funds will be liable to flow out in a massive way if the German economy shows signs of trouble. In this respect, the current-account deficit could no longer be ignored as an indicator of unsustainable imbalances in the economy – a diagnosis confirmed by several other indicators, such as reduced competitiveness, squeezed profits and the progression of wages, labour costs and prices. The unusual position of the DM at the bottom of the EMS band and the massive support it was receiving from some Member countries was a further indicator and inducement to submit to the necessary discipline.

For all these reasons, when conditions in foreign exchange markets approached crisis level in early 1981, there was a clear consensus that a major change of policy priorities was required for internal as well as external considerations. The overriding short-term objective was to re-establish confidence in the DM fully and rapidly and strengthen credibility in monetary policy. The response of the monetary authorities was tailored to provide a powerful signal but, at the same time, to retain a large degree of flexibility, since it was uncertain how the market would react and hence how monetary policy would have to be adjusted next. Closing the normal Lombard window and activating the special Lombard facility seemed to meet both requirements, while emphasizing the exceptional and hoped-for temporary nature of the measure. But since the unsustainability of the situation was perceived as being essentially domestic and related to long-established trends in the real sector, it was regarded as imperative over the medium term, to improve the flexibility of the economy, enhance market forces and reinforce the incentives for private sector activity and investment. The government that came into office in 1982 thus launched a comprehensive programme aimed at diminishing the share of public expenditures in the economy, reducing the tax burden, and cutting the budget deficit.

Assessment

With hindsight, the German authorities, like other observers, have some reserva-
tions concerning the policy-handling of these two episodes. While the response of the
Bundesbank to the dilemma situation of *1977-78* seems to have been broadly appropriate in its initial phase, monetary policy may have remained expansionary for
too long in view of the buoyancy of the economy in 1978 and the abatement of
exchange-rate pressure in 1979. As a result, the "monetary carry-over" hampered the
fight against inflation after the second oil shock, and the credibility of monetary targets, if not of the monetary authorities themselves, seemed to be in danger of being
lost. More generally, monetary policy and domestic monetary conditions turned out to
be less flexible than expected, and the assumption that even a significant departure
from longer-term norms could be reversed before it affected prices and wages proved
in the circumstances too optimistic. On the other hand, it was shown that confidence
in a currency can turn around very rapidly indeed. In fact, the contribution to price
stability of the strong DM evaporated sooner than expected. On the fiscal side the
decisions taken during this episode – and notably the package of 1978 in support of
domestic demand – are more difficult to assess. On conventional measures, fiscal
policy was only mildly expansionary during this period. At the same time, public debt
was growing steadily in relation to GNP, and the share of government in the economy
– the highest among the seven largest OECD countries – remained broadly unchanged. Budget developments in this period may thus have largely achieved their
short-term objectives, but may also have served to exacerbate rigidities and other
structural problems, with negative repercussions on the longer-term performance
– internal and external – of the German economy.

In conclusion, it would seem that the policy-handling of the 1977-78 episode was
perhaps not sufficiently cautious, in the sense that the German authorities erred on
the expansionary side – especially with regard to the size and nature of the fiscal
stimulus. But this episode had a large degree of dilemma in it, and the task of policy
makers was not facilitated by the economic environment of the time: experience with
an over-valued currency and with floating exchange rates in general was still limited;
monetary targeting was practically in its infancy; the energy crisis had greatly per-
turbed the economy and increased the level of uncertainty; and the analysis and estimates available at the time seem now to have significantly over-estimated the
degree of unused capacity in the economy.

The *1980-81* episode was perhaps more complex since in addition to an element
of internal-external dilemma, there was a conflict between monetary and fiscal policy
and, above all, an overlap of short-term, predominantly monetary considerations and

longer-term, structural aspects. The exchange-rate crisis of early 1981 was essentially the sudden and short-lived reaction of the market to growing evidence of problems in the German economy, the perception that some of them were deep-seated, and the view that the authorities were not paying sufficient attention to them. These domestic tensions and imbalances had been aggravated by external shocks – such as the energy crisis – but they were fundamentally the result of a long process which, as noted, had started well before these two episodes and was in part the by-product of the growing role of government in the economy, the excessive demand-side orientation of fiscal policy and the persistence of budget deficits. While the origins of the structural problems besetting the German economy were not directly related to monetary conditions, the stance of monetary policy may, in view of the degree of domestic inflationary pressures, have remained too accommodating for too long. Hence, even on purely domestic grounds, by early 1981 *some* tightening of monetary policy was necessary and probably somewhat overdue. This, along with the need promptly to re-establish confidence in the DM, required a strong and credible policy reaction and prevented a full relaxation once external conditions improved. Moreover, at this stage, monetary policy found itself in conflict with fiscal policy which was still supporting demand. The stance and nature of fiscal policy was perhaps fully exposed only after this tightening of monetary policy. It gave a sense of urgency to the ongoing debate on fiscal consolidation and restructuring, but by the time this medium-term programme began to be implemented the external situation had long turned around.

Hence, from a short-term, tactical viewpoint, external considerations played a major role in the adjustment of monetary policy in early 1981 and may have imposed a degree of stringency beyond what was called for by domestic conditions. But there was no lasting departure from established norms. In fact, it can be said that the long-term course of monetary policy was basically unchanged over the whole period covered by these two episodes, despite occasional shifts in the relative emphasis on unemployment and inflation, and shocks – domestic and foreign – which caused temporary deviations from established norms and subsequent corrections and compensations. On the other hand, 1981 marked a watershed for fiscal policy and the role of government in the economy. The foreign exchange crisis certainly contributed to speeding up the decision-making process. But this had already been set in motion and the external situation was perceived essentially as an additional symptom of the unsustainability of domestic imbalances and as a further inducement to take the corrective measures which were required by the ultimate policy goal of non-inflationary growth.

In conclusion, even though external conditions and implications were always duly considered, and on occasion affected the timing of policy moves, from a strategic viewpoint domestic requirements were clearly over-riding in the formulation of

German economic policy. While in this episode the internal-external conflict may have resulted in a certain cost for the economy – mainly because of the role of monetary policy – in a longer-term perspective the impact appears more positive, since spurred by the external pressure the authorities laid the foundation for a medium-term policy approach geared to sustained economic growth.

Note

1. The interest rate on special Lombard loans was initially set at 12 per cent. At the same time, remaining administrative measures affecting capital inflows were largely abolished.

Chapter 5

France, 1981-83:
the dangers of being out-of-step

Introduction

This chapter deals mainly with the development in France of an unsustainable external and domestic situation in 1982-83. Analysis of that period is set in the context of the shift in thinking about the conduct of economic policy that was taking place in France in the late 1970s – a shift prompted partly by ideas which were developing abroad and partly in response to the previous, less serious exchange-rate crisis in 1976.

Until the late 1970s, France had the fastest rate of growth, after Japan, of the major OECD countries, averaging 1 percentage point more than Germany over the 1960-82 period. Its relative performance has however gradually deteriorated. Whereas GDP growth exceeded the EEC average by 1 per cent per year up till the first oil shock, that differential narrowed during the years 1974-82 and has since disappeared. Up until 1973 brisk growth was coupled with moderate inflation, comparable to the European average. But after 1974 the French/German inflation differential began to be a problem, with France's annual rate of inflation over the period 1974-82 being 2.5 times the German rate. Despite the gradual increase in unemployment, wages continued to rise steeply in both nominal and real terms up till 1983. Worsening price competitiveness entailed not only the gradual depreciation of the franc, with its inevitable unwanted effects in what was *de facto* a highly indexed economy, but also a squeeze on profits that was sharper than the average for France's main partner countries, Germany in particular. All these factors combined to undermine foreign trade in industrial products. Whereas during the 1970s France had on average succeeded in combining GDP growth that was faster than that of its main partner countries with a comfortably positive export/import ratio, a feature of the 1980s has been the rapid deterioration in the trade balance whenever domestic demand is more buoyant than abroad.

To contend with these mounting pressures, the authorities mainly relied on fiscal policy measures; however, the short-term economic management during the 1970s was consistently implemented within the longer-term objective of limiting the public sector deficit. As a result, France was in a much healthier position than its main partners at the beginning of the 1980s in terms of the public debt burden. Action to counter inflation was based on repeated price and income control measures, while monetary policy played only a back-up role in this respect. In a highly regulated financial system, the main instrument of monetary policy on the domestic front consisted, until the mid-1980s, in the containment of credit through direct quantitative restrictions. Externally, foreign exchange controls were generally more extensive and complex than in most other countries, even if their stringency varied in line with fluctuations in the external situation. The basic balance excluding authorised borrowing (or trade balance in popular perception) was seen as the autonomous part of the balance of payments, whose financing had to be covered by capital movements. Interest rates were fixed by the authorities, external considerations playing an essential part in this process, even if the separation of the Euro-franc market allowed a certain autonomy, at least in the short term, in the event of speculative attacks against the franc.

The quest for greater interest rate policy independence – plus the pressures being exerted on the exchange markets – caused the authorities to leave the European monetary snake between 1974 and July 1975, and then again as of March 1976. But the French franc was again linked to the Deutschemark with the introduction of the European Monetary System (EMS) in March 1979; and during the 1982-83 balance-of-payments crisis, priority was given to remaining within the Community institutions.

The episodes

Despite the 1973 oil shock, growth remained strong in the first half of 1974, prompting the authorities to bring in a plan to slow the economy down in June 1974. The effect of the oil shock was still not clearly apparent in late 1974, and action to combat inflation was further stepped up at the end of the year. The result was that in early 1975 the French economy had to contend with the twofold effect of the world recession and the stabilization plan. The slump in activity and the government's response were both sharp and rapid. Two amending finance acts were brought in to stimulate activity and these fiscal measures injected additional public spending equal to some 2.3 per cent of GDP into the economy in 1975. A large proportion of the extra expenditure was directed to boosting public as well as private investment, and aid to consumption was also specifically targeted. The budget deficit was to a large extent covered by money creation, and the money supply grew by 18 per cent between March 1975 and March 1976, not slowing until the second half of 1976.

Overall, economic policy proved largely pro-cyclical. The plan to cool the pace of economic activity in 1974 came at a time when the world economy was flagging. The 1975 stimulus to activity coincided with an improvement in the international environment and resulted in a rapid pick-up in activity. However, despite sharp fluctuations in activity during the years 1975-77, domestic demand was never out of step with international demand for a prolonged period, and this limited the impact of changes in economic policy on the external account. On the other hand, France's inflation differential with Germany began to widen appreciably from 1974 on; and as a result external competitiveness, measured in terms of relative unit labour costs, deteriorated by some 10 per cent between the first half of 1974 and the same period in 1976.

With the combination of an upturn in domestic demand and worsening relative prices, the visible balance (balance-of-payments definition) showed a deficit in the last quarter of 1975 following surpluses in the first three. The deficit widened throughout 1976, beginning to narrow again only towards mid-1977. Strong pressure on the exchange market forced the franc to leave the European monetary snake on 15th March, 1976. The franc's effective rate fell by only 3 per cent up till June (from January), but in July 1976 the franc weakened again and its depreciation reached 11 per cent (still from January). After further fluctuations, the franc was back at its July level by end-1976, and the effective exchange rate then changed very little up till 1980. The current account moved back into balance in 1977, following a deficit of 1 per cent of GDP in 1976, and remained in surplus in 1978-79.

The government reacted forcefully to the worsening of the external account in mid-1976, and the fall of the franc in July, using all the instruments at its disposal to bring the economy gradually back to stability. The measures to combat inflation introduced in September 1976 provided for a freeze on the prices of all goods and services from 15th September to 31st December, 1976. The call money rate rose by 3 points between June and October 1976. As a result of the lagged effect of the measures to stimulate activity taken in 1975, the budget deficit continued to grow in the first half of 1976, but the tax increases decided in September 1976 and a more favourable spontaneous trend in expenditure sharply reduced the deficit in the second half. The 1977 budget continued to have a rather restrictive effect on activity. Money creation to cover Treasury spending was nil from September 1976 to end-1977. To accompany external adjustment, the government also encouraged large enterprises to borrow abroad, annual flows of these "authorised borrowings" rising from FF 14 billion per year in 1974-75 to 23 billion per year in 1976-77.

Following the March 1978 Parliamentary elections, the government took further steps aimed at gradually reducing the general government deficit, while at the same time liberalising the price system. As a result the general government account showed a surplus in 1980, France being the only one of the seven major OECD countries to achieve this that year. Yet despite a slight tightening of monetary policy, a continuing inflation differential with France's main partners persisted, due essentially to continued strong wage growth. The socio-economic context was such that, beyond some slowdown in 1976-78, wage trends could not be lastingly controlled: unit labour costs in French manufacturing industry increased by an annual average 11 per cent between 1974 and 1982 compared with 5 per cent in Germany.

With France's membership of the EMS and the return to a policy of fixed exchange rates, external competitiveness (measured in terms of relative unit labour costs) worsened in 1979-80 by some 5 per cent. The effects of the second oil shock caused the balance on current account to slip back into deficit (0.6 per cent of GDP), following the comfortable surpluses posted in 1978 and 1979.

Despite the worsening foreign trade situation, the new government formed after the Spring 1981 elections took a series of measures in June 1981 to counter the recession. The stimulation to activity in 1981-82 consisted mainly of raising the minimum wage, sharply increasing social benefits and creating public sector jobs – the total cost representing a little under 2 per cent of GDP. These measures were permanent in nature, and this was a major difference between the expansionary policies of 1981 and those of 1975 which were more easily reversible. The other big difference lay in the fact that French economic policy was now out of phase with policies being pursued in other countries. The structural budget balance (as estimated by OECD), which had improved by 2½ per cent over the two years 1979 and 1980, deteriorated by 1½ per cent in both 1981 and 1982. Domestic demand grew by 4 per cent in 1982, whereas on average it was declining slightly in the OECD, and in Germany it fell by 2 per cent. Under these circumstances, more than half of the increase in demand had as its counterpart a fall in net exports. The trade deficit thus widened rapidly despite franc devaluations in October 1981 and June 1982, which belatedly cancelled out the inflation differential with France's main partners. The current deficit increased from 0.8 per cent of GDP in 1981 to 2.2 per cent of GDP in 1982, worsening further in the first quarter of 1983.

The plan backing up the devaluation of 21st March, 1983 therefore focused mainly on slowing French domestic demand, which consequently grew less than in the EEC and OECD every year from 1983 to 1985. This slowdown in domestic demand was achieved in part by cuts in public expenditure programmed in 1983, and reinforced by strict discipline with regard to public spending over the period 1984-87.

Even so the public sector deficit, which stood at 3 per cent of GDP in 1983, fell only slightly to an average of 2³/₄ per cent of GDP in 1985-87. The principal means for achieving a reduction in demand and inflation was the introduction of a wage norm which – though not binding in a legal sense – was in fact adhered to and remained in force during the period 1983-86. This policy succeeded in bringing the rise in unit labour costs slightly below the German rate from 1986 onwards. The new mechanism involved the government's setting a price norm for the year and wages being adjusted *ex ante* on the basis of that norm. Monetary policy was used to impart a further restrictive turn, relative to the forecast trend in nominal demand resulting from the application of incomes policy.

With the slowing of demand growth, the trade balance recovered very rapidly. Whereas the target had been to cut the deficit by half within twelve months of the devaluation, that result was achieved in 1983. Foreign trade was restored to balance by 1985.

The franc's real effective exchange rate fell by some 10 per cent between end-1980 and end-1985 largely on account of the rise of the dollar, but export performance remained relatively weak: the ageing of the productive system and the mismatch between French supply and demand led to substantial losses of market shares at a time when demand for French goods was growing less than world demand. To smooth external adjustment the authorities again encouraged the major enterprises to borrow abroad in the early 1980s, the government itself also borrowing. All in all, annual flows of authorised borrowings rose from FF 34 billion in 1981 to FF 84 billion per year in 1982-83.

Main policy considerations

The first episode in 1976 substantially altered the government's approach to economic stabilization and inflation control, the emphasis centering on three main points:

- First, it was essential to keep the franc exchange rate strong in order to reduce import costs and force enterprises to rationalise production;
- Second, there had to be positive real interest rates on saving;
- Third, costs had to be kept under control by means of incomes policy; it was, however, not until the wage norm introduced in 1983 that this idea could be put successfully into practice.

After France left the snake on 15th March, 1976, two additional propositions, which were to play an important role in the preparation of the 1983 adjustment plan, became established. First, it was realised that abandoning a fixed exchange-rate arrangement in favour of floating could only delay adjustment, and not avoid it; in 1976 it was not possible to avoid the autumn adjustment plan. Second, the scale of the adjustment was not reduced by floating, but might even have been greater than it would have with a fixed exchange rate.

Two developments, one dating from 1981 and the other from the oil price falls in 1983 and then 1985, have had a lasting effect on the French economy in the 1980s. First, the steep increase in real interest rates – particularly as of 1981 – which followed the tightening of monetary policy in the main industrial countries, acutely affected the investment capacity of the already highly-indebted French productive sector, at a time when firms' profit-earning capacity was declining; productive investment fell by almost 8 per cent during the four years ending in 1984, settling in 1985 at a level barely above that reached in 1973. Second, France succeeded in the 1970s, by means of a policy that emphasized the signing of major contracts, in quite substantially increasing its exports to the oil-producing countries and to developing countries that were borrowing in international markets. With the debt crisis that hit the non-oil producing countries after 1982, and oil prices falling in subsequent years, demand for French exports fell more than world demand during the period 1983-86. This double handicap weighed heavily on adjustment policy and made the 1983-86 recovery more difficult than in 1976-79.

Following the October 1981 and June 1982 devaluations, the franc came under renewed pressure in October 1982. Government economic experts very soon concluded that a change in economic policy was essential if the franc was not to be devalued at increasingly frequent intervals. What was more, the level of indebtedness and, above all, the rate of new borrowing appeared unsustainable. The adjustment plan was ready as early as December 1982, a fundamental two-pronged decision having been taken: growth of domestic demand had to be brought down below the rate of growth of demand in France's main partner countries, and wage cost growth had to be tackled directly. The plan was not implemented immediately, however, and the franc was not devalued until 21st March, 1983, after the local elections.

It was generally agreed that a change was needed in the stance of economic policy. Some members of the government were in favour of France leaving the EMS exchange-rate system. This was not because they supposed that this would make it possible to avoid restrictive policies. On the contrary, many people (remembering what had happened in 1976) believed that leaving the franc to float on its own would necessitate an *even more* restrictive policy. Those who subscribed to this option saw in it the possibility of greater freedom of action and a way of avoiding further step changes in the franc's parity – something which was politically not very desirable. In the end, the decision to devalue the franc and stay in the EMS was taken for reasons that were not only financial – the possibility of recourse to the various sources of finance provided for by the EMS – but also economic – the discipline imposed by membership of the EMS being seen as important in the fight against inflation – and political – France not wanting any doubt to be cast on its commitments towards the institutions of the European Communities.

Implementation of the wage "norm" had a remarkable impact on the French/German inflation differential and, in the opinion of the authorities, this result showed that the adoption of a wage earning target could reduce the cost of economic adjustment. However, this result was also achieved by applying an orthodox demand management policy which reversed the growth gap between France and its partners. The break that took place in 1983 thus seems to have been twofold. On one hand, French economic growth was almost 1 percentage point lower than average economic growth in the EEC over the period 1983-86 while, on the other, the French/German inflation differential (GDP deflator) was reduced from 6 percentage points in 1983 to 2 percentage points in 1986.

Among the various macroeconomic indicators, it is the evolution of the external accounts that in France has traditionally been the flashing alarm that signals growing disequilibria. Franc devaluations have usually been accompanied by adjustment programmes. Recently (in the last six or seven years), however, developments in foreign trade (rather than the current balance), and in inflation – in particular the French/German inflation differential – have become increasingly important factors in the assessment made by national observers and the public of economic policy as a whole.

An indicator that played a significant role in France is government or government-guaranteed foreign debt (banking-sector debt only being taken into account by the specialists). Disbursed external debt is defined as the cumulation of net annual flows of authorised borrowing and government loans in excess of one year, adjusted for exchange-rate changes. The first loans were authorised in 1974 and outstanding borrowing totalled FF 123 billion at end-1980, FF 205 billion at end-1982 and FF 451 billion at end-1983[1].

In recent years the budget deficit, which had on the whole been quite small compared with other countries, has also become a subject of concern to the government. In this respect, the end-1982 announcement by the President of the Republic that the deficit was to be held to within 3 per cent of GDP would seem to have done much to alert public opinion to the problem.

Assessment

During the course of the period covered by this note, France has had to contend with a twofold external constraint. Firstly, in view of the fact that French industrial structures were clearly adjusting less rapidly than those of certain other countries to changes in demand, France's export performance in terms of market shares has been less satisfactory in recent years than it was up to the mid-1970s.

Secondly, irrespective of this medium or long-term constraint inhibiting the growth of the French economy, the events of 1982-83 – and, to a much lesser degree, those of 1975-76 – give an idea of the pressures that can build up when a country's cyclical position or the policies underlying that position become very different from those of other countries. The intensity of this apparent external constraint is perhaps surprising: the exchange markets seem less tolerant of a current-account deficit in France than in certain other major or middle-sized countries, even though France's external balance-sheet position has generally not been particularly unfavourable. This may have been due to the fact that inflation was not well under control, and perhaps also to the apparent sensitivity of the authorities themselves to current deficits: the market anticipates their response and so tends perhaps to accelerate it.

In 1976 the fundamental circumstances of the French economy were not very different from those of other countries. The employers' associations were, however, beginning to be concerned about France's competitive position and wanted the franc devalued. Furthermore, this was a time when the regime of floating exchange rates was still at an experimental stage, and markets tended to have a polarised view of "hard" and "soft" currencies: speculation against the franc followed immediately in the wake of the fall in sterling and the lira. Once the franc was out of the snake, corrective measures have been delayed during a few months. The decision *not to* rejoin the snake, which, in the opinion of the authorities, no doubt necessitated more austerity than would otherwise have been required, was taken for two main reasons. First, it was thought that France should make more progress towards restoring macro-economic equilibria before coming back into the system. Second, France's foreign exchange reserves were low and, prior to the creation of the EMS, financing mechanisms within the European exchange-rate arrangements were insufficiently developed.

In 1983 France's disequilibrium, or at least the degree to which the economy was out of step with the international conjuncture, was much greater. The increase in the budget deficit in 1981-82 was caused by the adoption of measures aimed at support-ing demand, which were in line with electoral commitments. Naturally this did not make the measures any more acceptable to the financial markets. The 1981 and 1982 devaluations were not accompanied by sufficient policy measures; as noted above, once it had been decided that France would remain in the EMS, it was considered essential that the 1983 devaluation should produce the desired results, and the necessary measures – particularly regarding incomes – were duly taken. Since then, France has adopted a medium-term approach which is rather similar to that of many other OECD countries.

In both the periods considered here, there were a great many indices pointing to a worsening of the situation. On each occasion, political factors were responsible for a relatively long period of time elapsing between the problems being identified and appropriate countermeasures being devised. At the political level it was above all the pressures in the exchange market, reflected in a fall in reserves, as well as mounting foreign debt, that seem to have persuaded the government to act. The 1982-83 situation can more accurately be described as "unsustainable" than the situation in 1976, though then too the thrust of economic policy had to be changed in order to prevent the situation from becoming unsustainable. So more stringent measures were required in 1983 than in 1976, when the recovery plan rested on maintaining household purchasing power more or less constant. With public opinion, and the attitude of the unions in particular, having changed in the meantime, it was possible as of 1983 to consider measures involving some fall in households' disposable income.

Note

1. At end-1983 these loans were divided into direct government loans (FF 63 billion), government-guaranteed loans (FF 327 billion) and non-guaranteed loans (FF 61 billion). In 1984 gross non-bank debt in excess of one year amounted to FF 525 billion (12 per cent of GDP); net debt, claims subtracted, increased from FF 197 billion in 1983 to FF 229 billion in 1984. Following the improvement in the current balance as of 1985 and the fall in the dollar, gross debt in June 1986 totalled FF 454 billion; net debt at the same time was down to FF 140 billion, i.e. 2¾ per cent of GDP. Also in June 1986, foreign exchange reserves stood at FF 453 billion.

Chapter 6

United Kingdom:
the sterling crisis of 1976

Introduction

This chapter focuses on the specific events and broader economic processes that led up to the sterling "crisis" of 1976 and subsequent changes in United Kingdom macroeconomic policy, followed by the conclusion of a standby agreement with the International Monetary Fund.

This episode must be seen in the context of policies and events which took place over a period stretching back practically to the beginning of the 1970s and which witnessed a series of shocks unprecedented in recent history – the flare-up of commodity prices, generalised floating and the first oil shock. This new international environment sharply increased the degree of uncertainty and greatly complicated the task of policy makers. Many well-established policy rules and theoretical underpinnings seemed no longer valid. Policies had to be framed under the pressure of events and in a somewhat tentative way as the authorities were groping for new points of reference and operational guidelines. For instance, the potential dangers of floating, especially the risk of a spiral between depreciation and inflation, may not have been fully appreciated early in this episode.

The deterioration of the economic performance of the United Kingdom in the mid-1970s – notably in terms of real growth and inflation – was worse than the OECD average, a result apparently to be ascribed essentially to domestic conditions. At a time when a high degree of flexibility was needed to carry out the structural adjustment required by the oil shock and the related terms-of-trade losses, in the United Kingdom a lack of social consensus, periods of government with no clear majority, and belligerent trade unions – which called a number of disruptive national strikes – interacted to make it difficult to find the right balance for macroeconomic policy among competing objectives. In this context, and perhaps because the United

Kingdom, unlike certain other OECD countries, had had no traumatic experience with hyper-inflation in its recent history, the political and social resolve to tackle inflation was slow to materialise. As discussed in more detail below, up to 1976 the basic macroeconomic approach was to use fiscal policy to try to support real demand, while the fight against inflation was left almost entirely to incomes policy. The role of monetary policy is more difficult to characterise: normally it supported fiscal policy, but occasionally the interest rate weapon was used to counter undesired exchange-rate pressure. The exchange rate may have been seen primarily as a variable affecting output and employment and, despite the inflationary risk of this approach, it was generally allowed to depreciate to preserve competitiveness. The role of sterling as a reserve currency, however, affected the interplay between internal and external factors, first alleviating balance-of-payments discipline following the first oil shock and then, in 1976, aggravating pressure on sterling.

The episode

With an expansionary budget in 1972 and accommodating monetary policy, the United Kingdom, like other OECD countries, recorded a strong economic expansion in 1972-73. Unemployment fell to its lowest level in years (2.2 per cent) but when the first oil shock hit in late 1973 the current account was already deteriorating and inflation increasing. In November 1973, "stage 3" of the Conservative government's incomes policy brought into effect the "threshold agreements" – with very unfortunate consequences, as these agreements turned out to act as a fast-triggering form of wage indexation in the face of a negative terms-of-trade shock. A general election returning a minority Labour government followed the calling of the miners' strike in early 1974, but threshold agreements remained in place, triggering payments up until November 1974. Another general election in October saw a small overall Labour majority, and after the expiry of threshold agreements the government relied on voluntary wage restraint to fight inflation. Thus, while the economy cooled off in 1974 and real GDP actually fell, the rate of inflation soared to 15 per cent in terms of the GDP deflator, and the current account deficit widened to nearly $ 8 billion or 4 per cent of GDP. Domestic financial conditions deteriorated and the stock market dropped sharply, with one index falling by some 50 per cent from January to December 1974 (which was the trough). The current account deficit was practically all financed through an increase in liabilities to foreigners, essentially the result of borrowing abroad by local authorities and state enterprises under the foreign exchange cover scheme ("compensatory financing") and a build-up of sterling balances by OPEC and other foreign monetary authorities. The pound sterling, which had been allowed to float in June 1972 and had depreciated significantly until mid-1973, remained relatively stable in 1974. The public sector borrowing requirement (PSBR) increased from 5¾ per cent of GDP in fiscal 1973-74 to 9 per cent in 1974-75 and there was an increase in the ratio of general government expenditure to GDP from 42½ to 48 per cent.

Stagflation continued in 1975: real GDP fell for the second year in a row and unemployment rose to nearly 4 per cent. Inflation continued to accelerate (reaching over 25 per cent). Fiscal policy was little changed and left the PSBR very high but monetary policy was eased early in the year. The "corset" (a control on banks' liabilities), introduced in December 1973, was removed in February 1975, and the minimum lending rate (MLR) was reduced in several steps from 11½ in January to 9¾ per cent in April. But then it was again progressively increased to 12 per cent in October. Threshold agreements were terminated at the end of 1974, and a new "£6 per-week" incomes policy (which although voluntary was backed up by cash limits in the public sector and sanctions on employers) was introduced in July 1975. For the year as a whole, the current-account deficit was more than halved to $ 3½ billion, but capital inflows, including compensatory financing, were just sufficient to provide its financing and a rundown of official sterling balances resulted in a roughly equivalent decrease in gross official reserves (some $ 1½ billion). Sterling depreciated by nearly 10 per cent from end-1974 to end-1975.

In late 1975-early 1976, economic activity picked up moderately and the inflation rate dropped somewhat (but was still well above the OECD average). The current account deficit was further reduced, in the face of quickening expansion abroad. Unemployment, however, continued to rise. The MLR was cut in several steps from 12 per cent in November 1975 to 9 per cent in early March 1976. The last cut coincided with a sudden run on sterling which was followed by intermittent waves of selling pressure. Mr. Wilson resigned as Prime Minister in mid-March, and Mr. Callaghan took over in April. The Budget in April 1976 envisaged a PSBR of well over 10 per cent of GDP in 1976-77, including cuts in income taxes conditional on agreement to a second stage incomes policy. PSBR restraint was not forthcoming until the substantial measures contained in the July package, and soon after the stage II incomes policy came into effect. Sterling depreciated by over 10 per cent in the Spring and reached a record low for the time of $ 1.70 in early June. A $ 5.3 billion credit from G-10 countries was provided on the understanding that the Government would apply to the IMF if it was not repaid in December. In fact, most of this credit remained unused. After a lull of a couple of months strong downward pressure resumed in September. MLR was raised and by the end of September the Government had applied to the IMF. MLR was further increased to 15 per cent in early October – a record for that time – the pound reached its trough ($ 1.56) before the

67

end of the month, and the "corset" was reimposed in November. In December, the U.K. government signed a letter of intent with the IMF setting out fiscal and credit targets that formalised the shift to a significantly more restrictive macroeconomic policy[1]. The situation turned round sharply in early November and the exchange rate rebounded as private funds began to move back into sterling. The authorities intervened heavily, this time to prevent an excessive appreciation of the currency. As a result, the capital account was in small surplus for 1976 as a whole. With the current-account deficit reduced to less than $ 2 billion, a large rundown of official sterling balances ($ 2 billion) was financed through drawings from the IMF ($ 1.8 billion) and use of reserves ($ 1½ billion). The substantial depreciation of sterling over the year (17 per cent) resulted in a significant improvement of international cost competitiveness.

Heavy upward pressure on sterling and official market intervention continued in 1977, despite a sharp reduction in interest rates (the minimum lending rate dropped from 15 to 5 per cent). To help maintain control of domestic monetary conditions, at end-October sterling was allowed to appreciate. Its appreciation over the year as a whole approached 7 per cent. The current account was practically back in equilibrium, and massive capital inflows (some $ 15 billion) combined with further precautionary drawings from the IMF (some $ 2 billion) resulted in an impressive increase in gross official reserves (nearly $ 17 billion). Economic growth was moderate in 1977-78 and unemployment remained above 5 per cent. Inflation decreased progressively, reflecting the stabilization of the exchange rate and moderation in wage settlements. The PSBR was reduced from 9¼ per cent of GDP in fiscal 1975-76 to 6½ per cent in 1976-77 and 3½ per cent in 1977-78 (or 4 per cent excluding the contribution of the BP share sale).

Main policy considerations

The dominant aspect of this episode was the emergence of unsustainable internal imbalances, essentially as a result of domestic policies. Until the exchange-rate crisis of 1976, priority was given to real domestic objectives, primarily support of activity and employment. The fight against inflation was largely left to incomes policy. On the external side, exchange-rate policy was caught between two conflicting considerations. On the one hand, relative stability of the nominal exchange rate, given an inflation rate above the OECD average, would have implied an appreciation in real terms, with negative repercussions on output and employment. On the other hand, a depreciation of sterling would have aggravated the problem of inflation, particularly in view of the *de facto* wage indexation scheme in effect in 1973-74. Also, in 1975-76,

68

considerable importance was attached to incomes policies and there were worries that they might be unhinged by exchange-rate depreciation. While all these aspects were taken into consideration in managing the exchange rate, over the longer run a depreciation of sterling was apparently seen as the lesser evil, given the overriding priority of employment as the ultimate macroeconomic objective.

Demand management policy thus remained broadly expansionary practically until early-1976, despite accelerating inflation and a large current account deficit. Monetary policy allowed a large proportion of the growing PSBR to be financed by the banking system and, despite the "corset", domestic liquidity increased rapidly. Fiscal policy between 1974-75 and 1975-76 changed little in terms of the outturn of the PSBR as a percentage of GDP, but monetary policy was further eased in 1975 and early-1976 – a move considered by many as one of the proximate causes of the March 1976 run on sterling. This stance of policy in the early part of the episode must however be seen in the context of that time, and the widespread view, held particularly strongly in the United Kingdom, that owing to their special character "oil deficits" had to be largely accepted (i.e. financed) until structural changes and longer-term corrective measures would reabsorb them. Similarly, it was widely acknowledged that to avoid an excess of world savings and a global recession, oil-importing countries should support domestic demand as much as possible. On the domestic side, given the socio-political situation sketched above, pressure for public expenditure and defence of employment was hard to resist. Growth in the PSBR reflected not only deliberate policy actions but also a number of inflationary features and rigidities embodied in the system. Furthermore, the monetary authorities in 1974 were much concerned with the state of corporate finances, which militated against any decisive tightening of monetary policy.

These policies and institutional features largely set the stage for the run on sterling of 1976, but tensions and imbalances were greatly compounded by external factors. Some of them – like the oil shock and the general increase in commodity prices – were clearly outside the control of the United Kingdom authorities, but others – like compensatory financing, the exchange rate and even the role of sterling as a reserve currency – were, in varying degrees, the responsibility of the authorities. Foreign currency borrowing by the public sector under the exchange cover scheme seemed for a few years to offer a way around traditional balance-of-payments discipline: as the creditworthiness of the United Kingdom was excellent, this technique could assure the financing of some of the current account without a need to raise domestic interest rates. The knowledge that North Sea oil was forthcoming may possibly also have contributed to official willingness to finance the deficits. Official sterling balances seem to have been a major determinant of both the size and timing of the exchange-rate crisis. For a couple of years, the tendency of a number of OPEC countries with

69

strong economic and political ties with the United Kingdom to invest a large proportion of their surplus oil funds virtually automatically in sterling provided a buffer for the current account deficit, masked the vulnerability of the United Kingdom external position, and reduced the pressure to adjust.

By early 1975, the United Kingdom economic situation was apparently already perceived by the authorities as being unsustainable. Their primary concern was with internal imbalances, essentially inflation and the PSBR. They thus started a process of reshaping incomes policy and fiscal policy with a view to gradually correcting these imbalances. In addition the authorities seem to have felt by late 1975 that a significant further depreciation of sterling was desirable – possibly necessary – to offset more fully the unfavourable inflation differential, restore competitiveness, and boost demand and output.

What exactly precipitated the first run on sterling in March 1976 and the subsequent waves of pressure remains a question of some controversy. It can be argued that market sentiment had already begun to turn against sterling in 1975. Despite a narrowing current account deficit, private capital inflows progressively dried up and official sterling balances began to decline. (The sterling guarantee arrangements had expired at end-1974, and in October 1975 Kuwait announced that it would no longer accept sterling in payment for oil.) From this perspective, the exchange-rate shock came surprisingly late. It is also argued that the timing of the shock reflected market perceptions that the Bank of England was actively seeking to bring down the exchange rate, though there is no evidence that such actions were actually taken by the authorities. Still others assign a particular importance to decisions by certain holders of sterling balances. If stepped-up liquidation of sterling balances was not the trigger, it certainly greatly accentuated the pressure, not so much because of the amounts directly involved but because it received a lot of publicity and provided a powerful signal to private investors. Sterling soon fell below a level considered appropriate on competitiveness grounds but, due to a lack of resources, a credible defence through official intervention was hardly possible. Official reserves were at a low, and a massive loan from international markets at that stage might well have carried conditions unacceptable to the United Kingdom since they would have sanctioned a loss of creditworthiness.

During 1976, the exchange-rate crisis escalated into a general crisis of confidence affecting practically all facets of economic policy. Under the pressure of events a new policy strategy was put into place. Monetary policy and notably interest rates were assigned the most immediate task of defending the exchange rate and giving the market an unequivocal signal of the overriding priority of this objective. Inflation was to be tackled through a more stringent form of incomes policy combined

70

with further cuts in the PSBR, scheduled over a few years. Reference to the expected growth of the money supply was explicitly made for the first time. Finally, the agreement with the IMF later that year was supposed to assure the credibility of the entire policy package through the customary IMF "seal of good housekeeping". Moreover, if exchange-rate pressure had not turned around as fast as it did, IMF drawings would have provided the resources for repaying that part of the G-10 loan that had been drawn and possibly financing further market intervention. Finally, the discipline of the IMF was probably deemed useful for the implementation of socially and politically contentious policies like those decided upon in 1976.

In terms of fiscal policy and incomes policy, the changes which took place as a result of the events of 1976, while important, were more an accentuation of trends already underway than a break with the past. On the other hand, the tightening of monetary policy and the announcement of a monetary target, clearly represented a quantum change: along with the involvement of the IMF it was seen by the market as a watershed, and may have been the key factor responsible for the rapid regain of confidence. This in turn allowed the authorities to lower interest rates substantially within a few months. But norms for the expansion of domestic credit and monetary targets remained in force. Along with the tightening of fiscal policy and incomes policy they continued to affect the economy well after this episode.

Assessment

With hindsight, few would dispute that by early 1975 the situation was unsustainable and that it was primarily domestic unsustainability of domestic origin. The deep-seated causes of the problem, as noted, were probably a complex interplay of socio-political factors. But the more proximate cause was the policy of trying to support real demand at levels which were excessive in view of the failure of incomes policy to contain inflation. Especially after the oil shock, too much emphasis was put on preserving economic activity and the standard of living, and because of the "threshold agreements" the first-round or mechanical impact of higher oil price was compounded by large increases in nominal wages. As a number of other OECD countries adopted a more cautious approach, the United Kingdom may have been somewhat out of line with the international business cycle, with negative implications for its current-account position. The nature of the fiscal stimulus was also largely inappropriate. The sizeable increase in the PSBR over the 1972-74 period stemmed too much from an increase in wages in the public sector, and too little from a reduction of social contributions for private industry – which would have been a way to

71

reduce costs and preserve disposable personal income despite the large terms-of-trade loss. In the event, costs increased and profits were squeezed.

The handling of the external sector was also open to question. Even allowing for the special character of the current account deficit, financing was, on balance, excessive and adjustment insufficient. First, foreign currency borrowing by the public sector started well before the oil shock and combined with the rapid build-up of official sterling balances, for a time greatly exceeded the oil-deficit component of the U.K. balance of payments. Second, since depreciation was seen primarily as a way to support output and employment, rather than as part of the adjustment process, it was not accompanied by the necessary reorientation of domestic policies. Hence, the progressive slide of sterling contributed to inflation, and little permanent improvement of competitiveness could be achieved. On both accounts, normal balance-of-payments discipline was largely avoided, which greatly increased the risk of a violent market reaction.

It is an open question whether the gradualist approach to adjustment already being implemented by the government by early 1976 could have succeeded if only the exchange rate had been handled more skilfully; or whether, alternatively, a more aggressive tightening of policy was necessary in any case. A more general question raised by this experience is whether in a regime of floating a country can engineer a depreciation of its currency without the process getting out of hand, especially when, like the United Kingdom in 1976, the country in question runs a reserve currency. The precise timing of the March run on sterling may well have been determined by specific factors or policy actions, but the apparent causality should not be over-emphasized. Financial markets are notoriously prone to discontinuities; that is, they often tend to treat emerging imbalances generously for a time, but then react suddenly and violently. In a way, the first stage of the currency crisis in early 1976 was only the tip of the iceberg. It probably got out of hand and snowballed into a full-fledged confidence crisis mainly because of fears of an uncontrollable spiral between depreciation and inflation. This forced the authorities to implement, and the unions and the country at large to accept, a policy package that entailed a major shift of priorities from defence of employment to the stabilization of the exchange rate and the reduction of inflation. At that stage there was, fundamentally, no longer any conflict between internal and external objectives, even though the need to "play it safe" and rapidly restore external confidence probably obliged the authorities to adopt a stronger and faster adjustment that they would have chosen on purely domestic grounds.

In conclusion, conditions were allowed to deteriorate for so long and become unsustainable either because the inflationary consequences of expanding nominal demand were not appreciated – perhaps because of an undue faith in incomes policy – or because it was felt that given the socio-political situation it was impossible to really cure inflation by deflating demand. It may be true that the necessary measures could not be taken until conditions deteriorated to a crisis point and the need for remedial action, on the internal as well as on the external side, became evident. On a more technical level, there seems to have been an inadequately integrated view during this period of all the facets of the problem – including the exchange rate and supply side considerations – and insufficient co-ordination between monetary policy and fiscal policy. The introduction of targets for broad money in 1976 was, at least in part, directed to achieving some control on the PSBR and assure the necessary co-ordination between fiscal policy and monetary policy. In terms of indicators and forewarnings, the gravity of domestic imbalances was clearly portrayed by cost-price data well before 1976; and, due to their forward looking nature, an even earlier indication of possible future problems was provided by the near-collapse of stock prices in 1974. On the other hand, because of the role of sterling as a reserve currency, the special nature of "oil deficits" and prospects for North Sea oil, the assessment of the external position and its sustainability was less unambiguous. But the market eventually developed a strongly negative view, perhaps because it weighted actual conditions – notably inflation – more than uncertain longer-term trends and prospects.

Note

1. In fact, the letter of intent merely reinforced the change in policy that the government had already announced. This included: a cut in PSBR; a strengthening of incomes policy (second stage); and a non-accommodating monetary policy (framed for the first time in terms of an official guideline for money supply growth).

Chapter 7

Italy, 1975-77:
at the crossroads

Introduction

This chapter focuses on the specific events, and broader economic processes, that led up to the exchange-rate crisis of 1976 and the introduction by the Italian Government of a comprehensive stabilization package in the second half of 1976 – followed by the conclusion of a standby agreement with the International Monetary Fund in March 1977.

From the early 1970s, a macroeconomic disequilibrium began building up in the Italian economy. Despite strong fixed investment, productivity gains were substantially outpaced by wage increases, and labour costs rose sharply. As international competition prevented a parallel increase in prices, profits were squeezed and companies had to rely increasingly on borrowing to finance fixed investment. During those years, monetary policy was still used essentially to peg interest rates and assure a smooth financing of the public sector deficit. Italy had a relatively rudimentary financial structure, and direct controls were extensively used to achieve the desired creation and allocation of credit without putting undue pressure on interest rates. In this context, and also reflecting the close co-operation between the Bank of Italy and the Treasury, the financing of the persistent budget deficit did not create major problems. There was a moral/political "understanding" that to help in the financing of the budget deficit the Bank of Italy would buy the Treasury bills that were not absorbed by the market; until the first oil shock, however, the increase in Treasury securities in the portfolio of the Bank seemed broadly in line with the ultimate goal of monetary policy of supporting employment and preserving reasonable price stability. The role of government in the economy, or more precisely the share of public expenditure, expanded rapidly after the mid-1960s, rising from around 35 per cent of GDP in 1964 to over 40 per cent in 1973. This reflected primarily the growing importance of social security expenditure which had a rather negative impact on the economy: to the extent that it remained unfunded it enlarged the public sector deficit and, according to the Italian authorities, increased consumption; to the extent that it was funded, it increased the burden on firms and labour and, along with other factors such as union constraints in the "official" labour market and the interaction between accelerating inflation and a highly progressive tax structure, it encouraged irregular employment in small enterprises ("underground economy").

Domestic tensions and imbalances were still relatively modest in 1973, and Italy had not recorded a current-account deficit for ten years. Nonetheless, combined with other structural features – such as the openness of the economy, the dependence on imported oil, the degree of wage indexation, and the low level of official reserves – they made Italy especially vulnerable to the first oil shock. But the root cause of the underlying deterioration of economic performance which culminated in the exchange-rate crisis of 1976 was probably the uncertain political situation, the lack of social consensus and the power of unions which interacted to prevent effective use of macro-economic policy and timely adjustment. As discussed in more detail below, fiscal policy was actively used after 1973 to offset the deflationary impact of higher oil prices on domestic demand, despite rising inflation. Social security measures were further expanded in an attempt to preserve households' purchasing power in the face of the terms-of-trade loss. Public expenditure approached 50 per cent of GDP and the budget deficit widened sharply, to nearly 10 per cent of GDP. Its financing began to pose serious problems for the conduct of monetary policy and the defence of the exchange rate. Aware of the risk of a depreciation-induced inflationary spiral, the authorities tried as much as possible to prevent the lira from declining below levels justified on grounds of competitiveness.

The episode

The Italian economy was on a strong upswing when it was hit by the first oil shock in late 1973: the unemployment rate dropped to 5.3 per cent in 1974 but inflation accelerated (to 20-25 per cent in terms of both consumer prices and GDP deflators) and the current-account deficit widened sharply to $ 8 billion, or nearly 5 per cent of GDP. The external deficit was partly financed through borrowing abroad by commercial banks and state enterprises encouraged by the authorities ("compensatory financing"). Official borrowing also played an important role (Italy borrowed more than $ 5 billion, mainly from the EEC, the Bundesbank and the IMF). As a result, net official reserves decreased by over $ 4½ billion but gross reserves actually increased by over $ 1 billion. The lira, in effective terms, depreciated by nearly 15 per cent during 1974, and international competitiveness remained broadly unchanged.

Throughout 1974 economic policy was progressively shifted towards a decisively restrictive stance, at a time when demand was falling in several major OECD countries. The result was the deepest recession in Italy since the early 1950s, with a drop in real GDP in 1975 (3.6 per cent) greater than in its trading partners. Price pressure appeared to ease but the fall in production was accompanied by a sharp progression in unit labour costs. Wages continued to increase rapidly as a result of pay rises and owing to the comprehensive system of automatic cost-of-living adjustment negotiated in January 1975. At the same time productivity fell. The current-account deficit was almost entirely erased, largely reflecting a steep reduction of imports. Thanks to private capital inflows, Italy was able to repay some of its outstanding official borrowings. (A $ 500 million loan from the Bundesbank was rapaid in advance.) The lira was practically unchanged in effective terms and international competitiveness deteriorated somewhat.

Monetary and fiscal policy was eased from the beginning of 1975. Short-term interest rates were reduced and export refinancing was increased and made less expensive. The Italian economy made an extremely rapid recovery as from the Autumn of 1975. But the Treasury financing requirement widened unexpectedly in the fourth quarter of that year and was met by the issue of a large volume of short-term paper which greatly increased the secondary liquidity of commercial banks. The monetary base also expanded rapidly. This was accompanied by a marked deterioration of the current account from the fourth quarter of 1975 onwards, as imports rebounded in line with the recovery in stockbuilding and in domestic activity in general. Combined with private capital outflows, this resulted in a foreign exchange "crisis" in early 1976. Despite sizeable official intervention (financed first through a run-down of gross reserves and then through new borrowing from the Bundesbank, the Federal Reserve and the European Community) the lira depreciated by over 20 per cent in the first four months of the year. (The official foreign exchange market was closed and intervention was suspended from late January 1976 until the beginning of March.) No longer being held down by a low level of demand and a stable exchange rate, inflation accelerated again.

The fall in the exchange rate and the loss of reserves caused a new tightening of fiscal policy, monetary policy and exchange controls. The discount rate, which had been raised from 6 to 8 per cent in February, was hiked by 4 percentage points to 12 per cent at mid-March; compulsory bank financing in foreign exchange for advance settlements of imports was reintroduced along with a compulsory non-interest-bearing deposit of 50 per cent on all payments abroad; and exchange controls, particularly on the export of currency by Italian residents, were tightened and more strictly enforced. The situation improved for a few months and the lira rebounded somewhat, but in the second half of September it came under renewed pressure. In October the discount rate was raised to 15 per cent, and the new government began the implementation of a comprehensive stabilization package aiming at tackling directly the imbalances in the real economy rather than simply palliating their monetary effects. But in view of the urgency of the situation, further specific measures, in addition to a general tightening of monetary and fiscal policy, were taken to improve the balance of payments[1]. In March 1977, Italy reached an agreement with the IMF and obtained a loan of $ 530 million; it also obtained a further loan from the European Community.

Starting in late 1976, the external situation and especially the capital account turned around rapidly once again. Due to large inflows in the fourth quarter, mostly in the form of trade credits to finance imports in response to the measures mentioned above, the capital account was in large surplus (over $ 4 billion) for 1976 as a whole, and Italy regained net official reserves (over $ 1 billion). In 1977, the current account also moved into a surplus ($ 2½ billion) and net official reserves increased by nearly $ 6 billion. Economic growth dropped to around 2 per cent in 1977, from nearly 6 per cent in 1976, and the unemployment rate rose to over 7 per cent. Inflation remained high until mid-1977 but eased considerably thereafter, reflecting a marked slowdown of import prices, the partial budgetisation of social security contributions, and a significant weakening of the wage-indexation mechanism (the government in early 1977 decided to limit the effect of increases in indirect taxes in the calculation of cost-of-living adjustments or "scala mobile"). The exchange rate settled on a mild downward trend: in effective terms, the lira depreciated by 7 per cent from end-1976 to end-1977, compared to 21 per cent the previous year.

Main policy considerations

In the couple of years from the first oil shock to the outbreak of the currency crisis in early 1976, the conduct of macroeconomic policy was affected by contrasting considerations. On the one hand, there was a growing perception, especially on the part of the monetary authorities, that the fundamental disequilibria which had been slowly building up at the macro and microeconomic level had been greatly aggravated by the increase in oil prices, and that this required extensive structural changes. But there was little or no consensus on actual corrective measures. On the other hand, as a result of the recession of 1975, there was broad agreement and strong pressures for a more expansionary economic policy. In the event, priority was largely given to protecting economic activity, the level of employment, and the standard of living. This orientation of policy must be seen in the rather exceptional context of that time. Internally, the country was suffering from a deep social malaise, affecting practically all segments of society and all forms of activities, and resulting in unsettled conditions on the shop floor, a high degree of labour absenteeism, as well as more extreme manifestations, such as terrorism. Hence, fiscal policy was basically used to preserve social peace; and to offset the impact of the terms-of-trade loss caused by the oil shock, social security payments were increased. As this measure became practically irreversible, it injected into the system an additional structural rigidity. Despite their profound conviction that the maintenance of employment and incomes by inflationary means would cause further distortions and could be no more than a stop-gap, the monetary authorities nonetheless accommodated this policy and the resulting budget deficit in view of the seriousness of the situation. The same considerations also motivated the decision of the employers' association in early 1975 to accede to the request of the unions for a greatly increased indexation of wages (the "scala mobile").

The decision of the Italian authorities in 1975 to stimulate the economy was broadly in line with calls from international organisations and European institutions on industrial countries to take steps to boost demand. Also, the international consensus was that, owing to their special character, "oil deficits" should be accepted (i.e. financed) until structural changes and longer-term corrective measures would reabsorb them. Italy relied heavily on "compensatory financing", and this combined with cyclical factors masked the growing underlying weakness of the external sector. The apparent strength of the current account seemed to imply that there was no major conflict between internal and external objectives or need for depreciation of the lira. Moreover, the authorities were well aware that a depreciation would fuel inflation, while a period of economic recovery could improve productivity and increase international competitiveness through a reduction of unit labour costs.

Hence, when the lira came under pressure in early 1976 the authorities tried, at first, to resist its decline. But Italy had surprisingly little room for manoeuvre. Gross reserves, excluding gold, corresponded to less than one month of imports. Gold amounted to some $ 12 billion, at market prices, but could not be easily mobilised. As for compensatory financing, the authorities had practically stopped using it in 1975, apparently judging excessive the risk of exchange-rate losses that it entailed. Moreover, late that year, the rumour spread that "...one of the American banking supervisory agencies was making a critical reassessment of lending to Italy"[2]. As a result, Italy effectively lost access to international credit markets, and compensatory financing could no longer be considered, even as an option of last resort. This left borrowing from foreign official institutions as the only source of finance, but it turned out to be less readily available than anticipated. The subsequent decision to close temporarily the official exchange market and stop intervening was meant not only to economise reserves but also to test the market and draw attention to the seriousness of the situation. However, since it was still impossible to form a government with sufficient political strength to take the necessary corrective measures, confidence deteriorated and the fall of the lira accelerated, threatening to go well beyond what was warranted by considerations of competitiveness. The authorities had to resume intervening while at the same time introducing a series of measures – essentially technical and *ad hoc* – to stem the net outflow of funds.

It was not until the Autumn of 1976 that the conditions necessary for a correction of the fundamental disequilibrium besetting the economy were finally in place. Following the June elections, a new government (headed by Mr. Andreotti) was formed, and an understanding was reached with the Communist Party allowing it to be associated, even if only informally, with the political decision-making process. At the same time, several months of nearly continuous crisis, a new run on the lira in September, and the spectre of an endless depreciation-inflation spiral had convinced practically all segments of society that the situation was unsustainable and that drastic changes were required, including actual reductions in real wages and living standards. These changes centred around fiscal policy which was the most conspicuous aspect of the disequilibrium. Monetary policy and interest rates also played a major role in the stabilization package, as is often the case when domestic unsustainability is combined with a currency crisis. But unlike in other such episodes, here the powerful signalling effect typically required to restore confidence and turn market expectations around was provided by the tightening of fiscal policy. The degree of wage indexation does not seem to have been greatly reduced at that stage: but the apparent willingness of unions to relinquish, even if only marginally, past gains may have had an important psychological impact, especially on inflationary expectations. In any case, in early 1977, feeling that negotiations between the trade unions and the employers' association (Confindustria) had failed to tackle the problem of indexation and labour costs as required by the gravity of the economic situation, the government legislated a major weakening of the indexation mechanism and introduced tax penalties to discourage supplementary wage increases at company level.

Although the IMF did not play a major direct role in this episode, the conclusion of a standby agreement was probably a necessary ingredient of the stabilization strategy. First, the customary IMF "seal of good housekeeping" was counted upon to assure the credibility of the entire policy package. Second, had the external situation not turned around as fast as it did, the IMF would have provided the indispensable resources to finance further market intervention. This point was still valid in March 1977 when the agreement with the IMF was reached and funds were already moving into Italy: in fact, some of the most effective corrective measures with respect to the balance of payments were supposed to be only temporary, and the degree of uncertainty was still very high. Finally, the discipline of the IMF was probably deemed useful for the implementation of unpopular economic policies – an arduous task, especially once the sense of urgency provided by the exchange-rate crisis had waned.

Assessment

There can be little doubt that the economic situation in 1976 was unsustainable, both internally and externally. The origin of the problem was essentially domestic. The long list of proximate causes included: a budget deficit that supported an excessive level of domestic demand and fuelled inflation; high real wages and unit labour costs that squeezed profits and investment; and institutional rigidities and structural problems. But the first oil shock and the usual interplay between internal and external variables – in this case, essentially the exchange rate and inflation – greatly accelerated the build-up of micro and macro disequilibria. In essence, the country refused the reduction in incomes implied by the terms-of-trade loss it had suffered. The run on the lira was thus only one aspect of a general economic problem which in turn was part of a socio-political crisis perhaps unprecedented in post-war Italy. Because of the deep-seated and exceptional nature of some of its ultimate causes, a correction of the fundamental disequilibrium besetting the economy required as a precondition the resolution of the political stalemate and a degree of social consensus to redress past excesses. It proved impossible to fulfil these requirements until conditions reached a crisis point, and the need for remedial action became evident to and accepted by a large segment of society. For all these reasons this episode stands out as rather exceptional and probably largely unrepeatable.

On a more economic level, the vulnerability of the balance-of-payments position and the underlying conflict between internal and external objectives was somewhat masked by the extensive use of compensatory financing in 1973-74, and the impact of cyclical factors on the current account until late 1975. And because of normal time-lags in the availability of data, the authorities were not fully aware in early 1976 of the deterioration of the trade balance that was taking place, and the outbreak of the exchange-rate crisis caused some surprise. On the internal side, while monetary indicators – and especially the rapid progression of the monetary base – should have been seen as evidence of worrying and possibly unsustainable developments, inadequacies in the timeliness and quality of data available to the authorities may have delayed this recognition. Indeed, in the following two years considerable attention was given by the authorities to the improvement of the monetary statistics.

Although the ceiling on bank lending was not operational from April 1975 to November 1976, Italy had a number of direct controls, notably in the financial sector, and the authorities may have felt that they had sufficient policy instruments to prevent the situation from getting out of hand. But the experience of 1976 proved that such controls rapidly become powerless in the face of a permanent macro-economic disequilibrium. More generally, this episode showed that monetary policy tends to lose its effectiveness when the economy is flooded with liquidity and in the absence of co-ordination with fiscal policy. The episode also underlined the dangers of a situation characterised by a low level of readily-available official reserves, little or no access to external credit, and a comprehensive wage-indexation scheme. Under these conditions it might be difficult to finance erratic speculation and even seasonal disequilibria, with the risk of an unwarranted exchange-rate depreciation and self-fulfilling destabilizing expectations. But it is nonetheless striking that one of the major countries, with practically no external debt, could come so close to exhausting all its financing possibilities. Excluding the official gold stock (which, as noted, was worth some $ 12 billion at market prices) the overall net external debt of Italy reached some $ 10 billion (5 per cent of GDP) at end-1976, compared to $ 5 billion in September 1975. In view of the drying up of foreign financing, the Italian authorities regarded this debt and its progression as an indicator of the unsustainability of the external situation.

A striking aspect of this episode was the important, if not crucial, role of political considerations. While any such assessment is inherently highly speculative, it seems that political considerations were determinant both in the build-up of the crisis and its correction. At first, gains scored by the Italian Communist Party in the elections of June 1975 and June 1976, and the possibility that this party might join the Government increased the degree of uncertainty and apprehension, at least in some quarters, made labour unions more belligerent, and encouraged capital flight. These developments might also have contributed to the rumours of a reassessment of lending to Italy by one of the American banking supervisory agencies noted above, and to the effective exclusion of Italy from international credit markets. Subsequently, however, the informal agreement with the Andreotti Government allowing the Communist Party to share in the responsibilities of government turned out to have a very powerful stabilizing effect. It provided the corner-stone around which Italy could finally or-ganise its strategy to tackle its many interrelated problems: a programme of economic austerity was introduced and rigidities began to be reduced; unions became more responsible; labour absenteeism and conditions on the shop floor improved; and ter-rorism was isolated and fought more effectively. Hence, in many respects 1976 proved a turning point. But while credibility in the economic authorities and con-fidence in the lira were restored very rapidly, and the current account moved into surplus as early as 1977, the correction of internal economic tensions and disequilibria proved, after a promising start, to be a more intractable and longer-term task, especially with respect to the budget deficit. A first round of reductions in the deficit due to higher indirect taxes was not followed by further significant reductions as the bulk of the increase in expenditure in the years preceding the 1976 crisis had taken the form of social security measures, which proved largely irreversible. Inflation and labour costs also remained a problem well after 1976. On the other hand, other internal economic disequilibria and tensions did show a significant improvement and eventually the performance of the Italian economy also improved.

Notes

1. These included: a temporary 10 per cent import deposit requirement and a 10 per cent tax on purchases of foreign exchange by residents; ceilings on bank loans made in lira; and the increase from 30 to 50 per cent of the required conversion of export earnings into lira that had been imposed earlier in the year.

2. "Report of the Year 1975", Bank of Italy, p. 195.

Chapter 8

Canada, 1981-84:
living in the shadow of the giant

Introduction

This chapter deals with the period 1981-84, which seems to offer a particularly good illustration of how international interdependence impinges on the Canadian economy and of the related problems of keeping policies on a sustainable path.

Trade between Canada and the United States is greater than that between any other pair of countries. Current-account transactions in each direction with the United States account for about 20 per cent of Canada's GNP. Direct investment and financial linkages are correspondingly close, and capital movements are fully liberalised. The Canadian dollar floats. Market judgments about Canada's policies and performance tend to be arrived at via bilateral comparisons with the United States. In these circumstances, Canada's policy options are inevitably circumscribed.

Over the decade 1976-86 annual inflation has on average been about 1 per cent more rapid in Canada than in the United States. The Canadian dollar has declined *vis-à-vis* the U.S. dollar in most years, and by some 30 per cent over the ten years – a fall that has served to overcome not only the bilateral inflation differential, but also the apparent overvaluation of the Canadian currency at the outset. Because of its natural resource endowment, which requires capital-intensive exploitation, and its relatively rapid labour force growth, Canada has normally been regarded as a structural capital importer; over the past decade, the current account has on average been in deficit by about 1 per cent of GNP – a more negative position than in the early 1970s but a smaller deficit than in the 1950s and 1960s. The unemployment rate, which has in the past generally been in the same range as that of the United States, has in recent years been significantly above the U.S. rate.

From 1975 onwards, the Bank of Canada set gradually declining target ranges for the growth of narrow money, M1. It had considerable success in meeting the targets, but the results in terms of reduction of inflation were disappointing. By the end of the 1970s, increased attention was being paid to other indicators of monetary conditions. In November 1982, monetary targeting was suspended, as it was clear that M1 growth was no longer sufficiently well related to interest rates and total spending to be suitable as an intermediate target for policy. *De facto*, the exchange rate became the most important intermediate indicator for monetary policy, though no explicit objectives have been set either for it or for any other intermediate variables.

The episode

Over the 1981-84 period as a whole, the overall value of the Canadian dollar changed little: it was on a downward trend *vis-à-vis* the U.S. dollar, though a much milder one than that of any other major currency, and was therefore pulled up on an effective basis by the U.S. dollar's great strength *vis-à-vis* other currencies. Within the period, there were three bouts of sharp downward pressure on the currency.

The first, in *July-August 1981*, came at a time when the U.S. dollar was moving up strongly against most major currencies, and the inflation differential between Canada and the United States was apparently widening; the current account was in sizeable deficit (2¼ per cent of GDP for the first three quarters of 1981), largely related to the fact that up to that point the level of activity had been better maintained in Canada than abroad. Markets were concerned about actual and potential long-term capital outflows associated with the takeover by Canadian firms of foreign-owned corporate assets – the "Canadianization" aspect of the 1980 National Energy Program (NEP). Moreover, at the time it was widely thought that some government policies in Canada were headed in a different direction from those in the United States, where the new administration was committed to reducing the role of government in the economy (and was hostile to the NEP). Confidence was also being adversely affected by disagreements between Federal and provincial governments on energy and constitutional matters and by cutbacks in domestic energy production. From mid-July to early-August, there was a flurry of takeover activity; this was mostly in the petroleum sector and related to the NEP, but other sectors of the economy were involved too. Market participants became concerned, not only about the capital outflows implied by these transactions, but also by the consequences for future net flows of investment income: typical dividend yields on the assets being acquired were very much lower than the cost of the borrowings by which the acquisitions were financed – short-term interest rates stood at the time at about 19 per cent.

The Canadian dollar fell by 3 per cent in three weeks. This fall occurred even though a good deal of the downward pressure was taken by a sharp increase in short-term interest rates to over 22 per cent, some 4 per cent above comparable U.S. rates, and sizeable intervention by the authorities in the exchange market. In order to reduce the downward pressure on the currency, the Minister of Finance in late July publicly requested banks to restrain their lending to finance takeovers involving capital outflows. He also signalled that the government had no intention of extending Canadianization to sectors other than petroleum. His statement seems to have been helpful in improving market sentiment, and – along with the big jump in interest rates – in turning the market around. The exchange rate recovered quickly: takeover activity rapidly waned; short-term interest rates eased markedly in the United States, permitting a decline in Canadian rates too; the economy moved into recession and the current account began to improve markedly.

The second spell of currency weakness, in *May-June 1982*, also occurred at a time when the U.S. dollar was showing considerable strength. By this time, Canada was deep in recession. Interest rates had fallen from 1981 peaks, but were still quite high. The inflation rate was running well above the U.S. rate, and unemployment in Canada had jumped to a significantly higher rate than in the United States. The budget of November 1981, which introduced some measures of restraint, was implemented only after considerable modification and delay. In early 1982, there was a renewed rise in U.S. short-term interest rates, but Canadian rates did not follow; the habitual differential in Canada's favour even disappeared temporarily. An impression seems to have gained ground in the markets that policy in Canada was "drifting": that in view of increasing unemployment the authorities might attempt to lower interest rates and accept a significant decline in the currency; and that the June 1982 budget was liable to mark a shift of policy emphasis towards expansion. Thus, although the current account was now in surplus and corporate takeover activity was subdued, the Canadian dollar came under intense downward pressure in May and June, losing over 6 per cent of its value against the U.S. dollar in a few weeks.

The authorities allowed short-term interest rates to rise by some 2 per cent and undertook heavy intervention in the exchange market. Moreover, the budget was in the event perceived as not representing a shift to ease; indeed, the authorities intended it to be neutral, given the constraints imposed by economic conditions on the one hand and financial market concerns on the other. Together with the introduction of public sector wage and price restraint (the so-called 6/5 program), which sought to address the unfavourable inflation differential with the exchange rate very much in mind, this served to restore market confidence. Over the summer the exchange rate returned to its level of the early spring, and with U.S. short-term interest rates falling rapidly, Canadian rates were allowed to fall too, though with the Bank of Canada moderating the speed of decline.

1983 was a year of stability in the exchange rate against the U.S. dollar, which was itself moving up against most major currencies. The next bout of pressure on the Canadian dollar was *between March and July 1984*, when it again lost over 6 per cent of its value *vis-à-vis* the U.S. currency. At this stage, the current account was in steady surplus. Inflation performance was much improved; and both it and the growth of activity were closely in line with performance in the United States. Fiscal policy had been given a medium-term orientation in April 1983 (though it also imparted short-term stimulus), reaffirmed in February 1984. Interest rates, though much lower than earlier in the 1980s, were still high relative to inflation. But the short-term differential *vis-à-vis* the United States was around zero, and when U.S. rates started to move up again from early 1984, there was strong market pressure for Canadian rates to rise also.

This pressure continued intermittently throughout the first half of 1984. Over most of the period, Canadian rates moved up broadly in line with those in the United States but, as the Bank of Canada was seeking to moderate the rise, downward pressure developed on the Canadian currency. Attempts to moderate interest rate increases led to speculative positions being taken against the Canadian dollar, and the resulting downward pressure on the exchange rate (which the authorities sought to moderate by intervention) in turn intensified the upward pressure on Canadian interest rates. Early in July, the authorities finally permitted a sharp rise in money market interest rates. Short-term interest rates had at that stage risen by some 3½ points since the beginning of the year, and had opened up a 1½ point differential *vis-à-vis* U.S. rates. Shortly thereafter, U.S. rates started to decline again, and Canadian rates were permitted to follow, though with a significant differential being maintained. The Canadian dollar recovered only a part of its fall; it remained somewhat above its July low point for the remainder of the year.

Main policy considerations

The period as a whole was marked by unprecedented strength of the U.S. dollar against other currencies in general, associated in part with the unbalanced U.S. policy mix. As it was lagging behind the United States in bringing inflation down, Canada needed at most times to have a positive interest differential *vis-à-vis* U.S. rates. With U.S. interest rates both high and fluctuating, this posed problems for Canadian monetary management. Moreover, the business climate in the United States was

86

generally viewed as being much more hospitable than in Canada (the period in question corresponding broadly to that of the first Reagan administration). The U.S. Federal government was perceived as being pro-business and determined to reduce government intervention and spending, while the Canadian government was viewed as interventionist, less business-oriented, and less committed to fiscal restraint. Canadian labour, which is more highly unionised, was viewed as relatively strike-prone and difficult to work with.

Against this general background, the three bouts of currency weakness examined here seem to have had rather different (proximate) causes. The first can be attributed to provisions of the NEP that encouraged direct investment outflows and that put a high priority on non-economic objectives; and to concerns in the business community about the general thrust of policies in Canada – especially relative to those in the United States. The second occurred when there were doubts about the Canadian authorities' resolve to persist with counter-inflation policies. The third seems to be largely explicable in terms of the impact of rising interest rates in the United States at a time when Canadian policies and performance would not in themselves have called for policy adjustment.

In all three of the periods of weakness, the authorities took some of the pressure in higher interest rates and some in a decline in the Canadian dollar, and made some use of (sterilised) exchange-market intervention. There was some reluctance to see domestic interest rates rise and, initially at least, more of the pressure fell on intervention and the exchange rate. Intervention, however, was largely passive and could be characterised as "leaning against the wind": it was concerned with the short-term rate of change of the exchange rate rather than its level. It was recognised, of course, that intervention and monetary policy could not work at cross purposes. In general, as downward pressure on the exchange rate intensified, and as market sentiment became increasingly negative, interest rates played a progressively greater role in arresting or reversing the pressure. Once expectations became widespread that the currency could decline further, these fed directly into financial markets and placed upward pressure on domestic interest rates. When such a point was reached, there was little alternative but to take a good deal of the pressure on interest rates.

Markets became very sensitive to the dilemma that faced the authorities when U.S. interest rates rose (or were expected to do so) or when the Canadian dollar came under downward pressure. Indeed, despite the reactions described above, it was at times perceived that if the currency came under downward pressure the authorities would be reluctant to let Canadian interest rates rise, while if it came under upward pressure the authorities would take the opportunity to lower rates. As the Canadian dollar continued to follow a downward trend, the view became increasingly common that, in the event of a policy conflict, the authorities would find it easier to let the currency slide. Exchange-rate expectations became asymmetric: it was thought that the Canadian dollar could move down, but was unlikely to appreciate to any extent. In the event, there were indeed several downward "spikes" in the evolution of the currency, but no upward ones.

In the first two episodes, it proved possible to unwind much of the movement in all three "pressure" variables – the exchange rate, interest rates and intervention – once a significantly positive interest-rate differential had been restored. In the third episode, however, the currency did not recover much.

Throughout the period covered by this note, interest rates had to be kept higher than the authorities would have chosen on purely domestic grounds. They judge that rates could have been lowered had fiscal policy been tighter, but that this was scarcely a feasible option given the very high unemployment rate (over 11 per cent for much of the period). The authorities were thus constrained to "mimic" to some extent the policy mix in the United States: fiscal policy was looser than would otherwise have been desired, and monetary policy tighter.

Assessment

Canadian policies and performance were at no stage so far off a sustainable path that there was a need for the sort of major reappraisal of policies that has occasionally been required in some other countries. But although there were no major upheavals in macroeconomic policy, it was nonetheless a period of active policy-making: adjustments were required to what turned out to be the steepest post-war recession, as well as to market volatility in the face of high inflation and major international imbalances. There was a need for constant vigilance over financial markets. In particular, the authorities needed to act from time to time to ensure that policy would continue to be perceived as giving high priority to the domestic and external value of the currency.

Whenever a downward movement in the Canadian dollar began to gather momentum it became increasingly clear that domestic interest rates would have to rise, in the absence of interest rate declines in the United States. As the currency moved down, the demand for Canadian-dollar-denominated interest-bearing assets weakened; had the authorities sought actively to hold Canadian interest rates down in these circumstances, an unstable situation would probably have developed, characterised by a further fall of the currency, intensification of inflationary pressures, and eventually still higher interest rates. In this sense, the pre-existing level of short-term interest rates and differentials could be said to have become unsustainable.

Thus there was probably no realistic option of taking sharp downward currency pressure virtually entirely on the exchange rate itself, in the hope that in due course this would permit a lower level of domestic interest rates once market participants expected an appreciation of the currency. This approach would have been risky, because of the extrapolative nature of short-run exchange-rate expectations when there is nothing to "anchor" them. Indeed, although it is difficult to draw conclusions about *ex ante* pressures from the *ex post* data, it appears that attempts to adopt this option would have been increasingly dangerous in successive episodes.

The Canadian experience over this period can perhaps be assessed at different levels. One possible reading is that the continual and evident need for policies to adapt to pressures from across the border, and notably for policy adjustments to avert the risk of the economy being plunged into a cumulative process of depreciation and inflation, prevented the emergence of unsustainable situations. At a deeper level, however, the assessment might be rather less sanguine. The tendency from 1976 onwards for the Canadian dollar to be a "weak currency" was attenuated but not, in the period considered here, eradicated. Although it is impossible to cite hard facts, it may be the case, not only that there was a risk premium on Canadian-dollar-denominated financial assets, but that this premium was increasing over time, thereby tending to raise the general level of Canadian interest rates. Furthermore, Canada emerged from the period under review with a fiscal deficit (at the general government level) of $6^{1}/_{2}$ per cent of GNP, too high to be sustained over the long term.

Chapter 9

Netherlands, 1975-82:
containing the public sector

Introduction

This chapter focuses on the reorientation of Dutch economic policy away from demand management towards a more market-oriented approach, a main element of which is budget-deficit control. This reorientation is directly associated with the coalition government of Liberals and the Christian Democratic Party of Prime Minister Lubbers, which came into office after the elections in 1982 – by which time both the budget deficit and the economic situation more generally had got so far out of control that the need for decisive action had become apparent not only to politicians, but also to labour unions and the population at large. Well before 1982, successive governments had attempted to come to grips with an economic situation that was increasingly recognised as unsustainable, but – in the absence of overt crisis conditions – action had been frustrated by the seeming impossibility of translating economic analysis into a course of policy that could mobilise and command sustained political support. The simultaneous explosion of the budget deficit and near doubling of the unemployment rate in the 1980-82 period may thus have been the necessary catalyst for action.

The problem – or nexus of problems – facing the Dutch economy in the 1970s has come to be called the "Dutch disease" – though the benefits of natural gas was only one of the forces shaping economic developments in the Netherlands during this period; and many features of the Dutch economic experience are reflections of trends that were common to a number of European countries – essentially linked to rising inflation, the rapid development of the welfare state and the associated explosive growth of government. Detailed analysis of the economic mechanisms operating during this period is beyond the scope of this note; in a very summary way, the following broad features of the Dutch economy and the economic policy regime in the 1970s might serve to set the context for the episode under consideration:

90

i) During the 1970s, it was decided that the benefits from gas reserves should be used largely for the expansion of the collective sector, rather than for strengthening the market sector of the Dutch economy. The substantial part of the rising gas revenues that passed into the hands of the government in the form of royalties, taxes and profits permitted broader and more generous social programmes, subsidies for industry and an increase in public services generally. By 1982 the Netherlands was second only to Sweden in the size of public expenditures relative to GNP;

ii) Growth of the public sector, however, can only be accounted for to some extent by gas revenues. The burden of taxes and social security premiums as a share of GNP had been rising by well over 1 percentage point per year since the mid-1960s, and continued to increase up to 1983 despite efforts from 1976 onward to restrain their growth. As explained below, a central problem in this regard was the impact on wage formation;

iii) Real wage growth in the Netherlands had exceeded productivity growth since the mid-1960s, and wage aspirations were slow to adjust to the slow-down in potential growth that was occurring – in the Netherlands as elsewhere – during the 1970s. Natural gas may have contributed to the persistence of strong wage growth to the extent that it raised measured aggregate productivity growth, which in turn was used as a guideline in the national wage bargaining process. As tax burdens rose, wage negotiations increasingly focused on after-tax earnings so that, given near total indexation of wages, the terms-of-trade deterioration of the non-energy sector and rising taxes and social premiums were essentially passed forward to enterprises. This engendered strong upward pressure on domestic prices. However, with many price increases limited by international competition and a strong Guilder, the result was a growing profit squeeze in the private sector. Resulting slower growth in private sector employment in turn generated pressure for further public sector employment, while wage-parity considerations also pushed up public-sector wages. The links between wages and social security benefits led to further expansion of outlays and premium increases. The resulting expansion of government necessitated further tax increases in a sort of vicious circle;

iv) Monetary policy throughout this period was primarily concerned to maintain the external value of the Guilder *vis-à-vis* the Deutschemark (the "hard currency option"). With inflation generally somewhat above German rates owing to diverging wage-cost developments, this implied a real appreciation of the Guilder *vis-à-vis* the Deutschemark, and an even larger one in effective terms up until 1979. External competitiveness, which had already suffered from the concentration of Dutch industry in energy-intensive sectors, was thus further impaired, though rising sales of natural gas kept the current-account in surplus until 1978 (and contributed to a restoration of the surplus in 1981 following the further rise in energy prices). The external surplus meant that monetary policy had relatively little scope to directly control domestic monetary conditions. From 1976 onwards, however, the domestic focus of monetary policy was to reduce gradually the excess liquidity that had built up in the previous year, with controls over domestic credit expansion the principal instrument;

v) Budget policy formulation was strongly influenced by the notion of a sustainable structural budget deficit. During much of the decade, it was considered that a structural deficit of around 4 per cent of net national income was consistent with the structural excess savings of the private sector and a small surplus on the current-account. Cyclical deviations around the norm were accepted, and indeed judged appropriate for demand-stabilization purposes.

The episode

As noted above, the primary symptom of an internal disequilibrium in the period from 1975 to 1979-80 was the inexorable rise in the size of government share in the economy and the corresponding tax burden. On the surface, other indicators gave less cause for alarm: output, led by relatively buoyant domestic demand, continued to grow at a steady rate of about 2½ per cent per year (following the bounce-back from the 1974-75 oil-price induced global recession). Inflation came down steadily from over 10 per cent in 1975 to just above 4 per cent in 1979. Unemployment remained steady at about 5½ per cent – high by past experience and thus a *prima-facie* argument for maintaining relatively expansionary policies. Yet within the government the perception that structural problems were building up was already quite clear (for instance, in the rapid growth of workers claiming, and obtaining, disability pensions). Internal projections made in 1976 clearly suggested the unsustainability of growing tax-burdens, and identified the linkage between tax-push, real labour costs, squeezed profitability, and eventually lower employment. The "1 per cent rule" adopted in 1975 – which limited future increases in the burden of the collective sector to 1 percentage point per year – seems with hindsight a relatively weak response and, in the event, was not strictly adhered to. This action did, however, imply a certain discipline relative to experience in the previous years.

The private sector employment consequences of rising real labour costs were slow to make themselves felt; recollections of labour scarcity up to the early 1970s may have made firms reluctant to shed labour. In addition, labour shedding was hampered by government regulations and the attitude of the unions toward company reorganisations. With unemployment stable, public awareness of the unsustainability of disappearing profits (by 1982 the net operating surplus in manufacturing had fallen to below 7 per cent of value added, compared to over 27 per cent in 1974) was also slow to develop. Indeed, within the overall policy debate, the counter-proposition that high wages were good for employment because they stimulated demand remained an important theme. It was supposed that such demand support would help Dutch industry get through the down phase of the business cycle, which was considered to be a temporary phenomenon. In this way the signals from the deteriorating competitive position of parts of Dutch industry were ignored, or even overruled. Subsidies to the weaker parts of industry indirectly impaired stronger companies; and this in turn led to an erosion of the earning base of the economy. The budget deficit, as such, did not become a focus of attention (until 1980), since the 4 per cent norm was not being egregiously violated and deficits were also seen as good for demand. (Furthermore, *ex ante* projections of sharply rising deficits were not realised *ex post*. This encouraged the view that the deficit was under better control than it ultimately proved to be. It also led to over-estimates of the growth effects of extra deficit-financed government outlays.)

What did become a matter of concern, from late 1977 onward, was the emergence of a current-account deficit. In fact the deficit itself never became very large – peaking at 1½ per cent of GNP in 1980 – and a surplus was restored by 1981. But this marked a considerably larger deterioration of non-gas net exports, and so served to intensify concern about the deteriorating profit position of enterprises and their loss of external competitiveness. The Guilder also came under pressure in late 1978 – necessitating sharp increases in short-term interest rates (to a peak of 24 per cent) to maintain parity with the Deutschemark. Devaluation as an option for dealing with the external competitiveness problem was never seriously considered by the government, given *inter alia* the large measure of indexation of the Dutch economy. On the contrary, the "hard currency option" was reaffirmed in 1978 – with a formalisation of the peg to the Deutschemark – and defended vigorously when the Guilder came under pressure again in late 1979. In addition, credit expansion was reduced by strict domestic ceilings. The external deficit, finally, served to focus increased attention on the budget deficit ("a hole in the budget is a hole in the current-account") – though this concern did not become generalised until later.

The response of the government to these concerns was "Blueprint '81" which was drafted in 1978. Its primary focus was not initially the budget deficit, but rather the restoration of enterprise profitability, employment and investment. Real wage growth was to be brought down to zero through a strengthened incomes policy, supported by increased government contributions to the social security funds to permit a reduction of social premia and thereby moderate labour costs directly. This made it easier for labour unions and employers to reach agreement in their wage negotiations; but the deterioration of the competitive position continued. Expenditure cuts were also planned for the 1979 budget to permit a stabilization of the aggregate tax burden. Industrial policy, finally, was reorganised with the aim of increasing investment by expanding the scope of government support to industry. With hindsight, this proved to be a policy with only limited success. The budget deficit problem did become of increasing concern over time (especially as – with the weakening of economic activity in 1979/80 – efforts at expenditure restraint were failing to be implemented). The 1980 budget broke with precedent by setting an absolute limit of 6 per cent of Net National Income to the deficit so that – when projections showed that this limit would be exceeded – additional spending restraints were implemented.

The years 1980-82 witnessed a remarkable deterioration of economic performance. The global recession that followed from the second oil crisis of 1979 was of course a key influence, but its impact was compounded by domestic factors: monetisation of the budget deficit, which had begun to increase in 1979, could not be allowed to continue without undermining inflation control and the credibility of the hard-currency option. Long-term real interest rates rose substantially, though less than in other countries, with strong adverse effects on investment. A three-year surge in participation rates (concentrated among women), coupled with a labour shake-out in the private sector (the long-delayed response to excessive labour costs) meant that the unemployment rate more than doubled over the three years – from 5.4 per cent in 1979 to 11.4 per cent in 1982 on the basis of the OECD's standardized measure. (Excluding the semi-collective sector, however, the deterioration of employment in the market sector can be traced back to the early seventies.) The budget, finally, got out of control under the impact of social expenditures triggered by the recession. Despite a rise of almost 4 percentage points in the share of government receipts in net national income (to 60.4 per cent in 1982 on the national definition) the government borrowing requirement rose to above 8 per cent, and was estimated in September 1982 to rise to 12 per cent in 1983. Although the need for action was clear, the capacity of the government to forge a response was hamstrung by a political impasse which was resolved through the 1982 elections that brought in a (relatively) unified centre-right wing government with a clear parliamentary majority.

The new government made budget control the overriding economic and political priority. Control of the budget deficit was judged essential because the consequences

94

of debt-accumulation for interest payments implied that the deficit was on an unsustainable course. But in putting in place the machinery for effective budget control, which required coming to grips with indexation mechanisms and open-ended spending programmes, the new government also aimed to achieve broader objectives of a supply-side nature – greater reliance on markets, restoration of profits, and a reduction of the role of government generally. This policy had broad public support, as people became aware that the weakening of the economy had taken on worrisome forms, and that structural elements had gradually become dominant. Doubled unemployment figures brought the unions down to earth. Indeed, over the following years, while a gradual reduction of the deficit was achieved (broadly along the path envisaged in 1982), the simultaneous stabilization and then reversal of the overall tax burden, a marked moderation in labour costs (at a time of government withdrawal from the negotiation process in the private sector) and restoration of enterprise profitability were equally, if not more significant aspects of the return to a more sustainable situation.

Major policy considerations

The complexity and largely structural nature of the difficulties facing the Dutch economy over the decade up to 1982 makes a comprehensive consideration of the policy choices over this period very difficult. Two issues of central relevance are briefly explored below: the first is the relationship between economic analysis and policy choice; the second is the hard-currency option.

The Netherlands has a long and well-developed tradition of using macroeconomic analysis and explicit medium-term scenarios in the process of economic policy formulation. On balance, this approach did generate useful indicators for policy over the period being considered. For example, the slowdown in potential growth of GNP that occurred throughout the OECD from the late 1960s onward was perceived and acted upon rather earlier in the Netherlands than in other countries (though even in the Netherlands there was a considerable perception lag). In 1976, and again in 1978 official estimates of potential growth were adjusted downward (from the 4½ per cent that had been assumed in the early 1970s to 3 per cent – which was still, as it turned out, somewhat of an over-estimate). Estimates of the "structural" component of the budget deficit were revised accordingly and – given the 4 per cent norm – this change may have forestalled the development of even more severe deficit problems. Similarly, by 1975 the core problem of rising real labour costs and its eventual implications for employment was clearly identified (well ahead of actual observed consequences on the labour market, and of international concern with the real labour cost issue).

As regards the role of the budget in the economy, economic analysis was perhaps less successful. The modelling framework in use up until the late 1970s clearly suggested that deficits were "good for demand" and hence would contribute to employment and output growth. Failure to incorporate "crowding out" effects through the monetary sector may thus have contributed to a bias towards fiscal expansion on Keynesian grounds during this period.

Yet the key difficulty was not one of economic analysis. At the level of analysis, it was already perceived in 1975 that the Dutch economy was moving onto an unsustainable course. That it took seven years for decisive action to be taken in response to this perception seems essentially a political phenomenon. The "1 per cent" norm of 1976, and the "Blueprint '81" programme launched in 1978 were both, in different ways, directed at the core problem, but in the absence of political consensus that "hard medicine" was necessary (and in the absence of popular perceptions that there was an urgent problem requiring changed behaviour – in particular in wage-setting) these programmes tended to be diluted by the pressure of external events or internal political disarray. Thus, in the end, it was only the emergence of visible crisis – and not the understanding that one was impending – that could provoke a decisive policy response.

The actual course of developments in the Dutch economy over the period considered was shaped to an important extent by the choice of an exchange-rate objective for monetary policy. The peg to the Deutschemark (approximate during 1975-78, and more rigid from 1979 onward) proved an effective instrument for inflation control, given the consistently anti-inflationary monetary stance of the Bundesbank. (In fact the Guilder did not fully follow the Deutschemark in the September 1979 realignment, and underwent an "inadvertent" devaluation *vis-à-vis* the Deutschemark in March 1983, in the context of another EMS realignment.) Whether this approach imposed avoidable short-run costs on the Dutch economy is perhaps debatable, though it is hard to imagine that an alternative approach would have yielded uniformly better results. It might be that a less rigorous peg, or one that focused on a basket of foreign currencies, could temporarily have alleviated somewhat the pressure on the manufacturing sector – but with a concomitant weakening of control over inflation and probably higher interest rates in the longer term. Certainly, given wage indexation and the extreme openness of the Dutch economy to trade, the squeeze on profitability and external competitiveness to which Dutch industry was exposed during the period could have been allayed only very temporarily by devaluation. In a sense, too, the issue was moot for much of the period because of the current-account

96

surplus. The emergence of the natural gas industry implied a squeeze on the international competitiveness of other sectors that would have occurred to some extent under any plausible exchange-rate regime. (The squeeze on the manufacturing sectors in those countries that benefited from North Sea oil can be taken as evidence for this proposition.) For the monetary authorities, the decisive consideration was interest rates. In the absence of a credible anchor for policy in the Deutschemark peg, inflation pressures would presumably have been greater, necessitating tighter monetary policy on domestic grounds and higher interest rates on average. By establishing the credibility of the hard-currency option in 1978-79 (which required, at times, brief periods of extremely high interest rates) it was hoped that the risk premium on Dutch interest rates relative to those in Germany could gradually be eliminated. In these terms, the policy has proved quite successful. It is for these reasons that the (small) 1983 devaluation of the Guilder against the Deutschemark is generally regarded as unfortunate; and indeed a risk premium reappeared in Dutch interest rates thereafter.

Assessment

From the perspective of sustainability, and the forces leading governments to take action in the face of an unsustainable situation, this episode suggests several lessons:

i) While advance indicators of an unsustainable situation were available, and recognised, well before 1982, it took a number of years for the actual economic situation to deteriorate to the point where action could not be deferred. The 1976-79 period proved to be one where, under mounting structural difficulties, the usual macroeconomic indicators (growth, inflation, unemployment) failed to bring out clearly enough the ongoing structural deterioration of the competitive position of Dutch industry. Gas revenues to some extent masked both the current-account and budget implications of this structural deterioration;

ii) The problems facing the Dutch economy, which burst into the open in 1980-82, had a number of different dimensions. Policy efforts to deal with these problems prior to 1982 may have been less effective than hoped because, in attempting to address the different aspects of the situation, no *single* clear overriding objective for policy could be established. The success of the new government in changing course in 1982-83 may in part be explained by the emphasis given to a single indicator, the budget deficit, as an objective around which political will (and cohesion) could be mobilised;

iii) The capacity of a government to act decisively in the face of an impending problem is to a significant extent constrained by perceptions and attitudes within the population at large – as reflected also in their political representation. To a considerable extent, preventive action was ruled out so long as the population did not clearly perceive that there was a serious problem. The dramatic deterioration of Dutch economic performance in 1980-82 may have been a necessary pre-condition for action because it finally mobilised a national perception of the need for it;

iv) Finally, it should be noted that the broader international climate of opinion, as well as domestic perceptions, played an important role in shaping the policy responses. If direct "peer pressure" on the Dutch authorities did not play a role in this episode, the shift away from an aggregate demand focus toward a more supply-oriented policy throughout the OECD in the early 1980s provided a domestic anchor for policy reform. Not only the intellectual climate (as embodied, for instance, in the main lines of the OECD's medium-term strategy) but the examples of more classical economic policy approaches being implemented in other countries were relevant in this context.

Chapter 10

Sweden:
the 1982 devaluation of the krona

Introduction

The 1982 devaluation of the Swedish krona by 16 per cent against the country's exchange-rate basket is one of the strongest measures taken in recent Swedish economic history. To some extent, it can be regarded as the most dramatic element of a gradual change in the economic policy response to the adverse development in Sweden's external environment following the oil price increases and the international slowdown of growth. The size of the devaluation could be seen as a reflection of the high level of ambition in Swedish economic policy, particularly the wish to avoid increases in open unemployment, which at a rate below 3.5 per cent of the labour force has remained among the lowest in the OECD area since the first oil shock.

Whereas Sweden's fiscal policy instruments are fairly traditional for an OECD country, monetary policy in most of the period leading up to the 1982 devaluation was pursued within a framework of very tight regulations on financial markets, making it possible for the monetary authorities to influence both prices (interest rates) and quantities (financial flows). One of the aims of this system was to secure cheap financing of certain activities – mainly housing investments, but the public sector also benefited from below-market interest rates. However, partly as a result of increasing public deficits this system came under increasing pressure in the period under consideration. As a result of this, and with monetary authorities favouring a change, the financial markets underwent a gradual transformation towards a more market-oriented system from around 1980 onwards.

Direct interference with decisions taken in the private sector has taken the form of regulations on e.g. lay-offs, and occasional price-freezes. Furthermore, during the period considered there was a blooming of different kinds of subsidisation schemes for a number of industrial sectors. Despite attempts to influence wage settlements through public statements and other indirect measures, there was no formalised incomes policy.

Partly as a result of fiscal policies to prevent a rise in unemployment, government employment has risen considerably (24 per cent of total employment in 1973 and 32 per cent in 1982) together with a number of employment and labour market schemes which, at their peak in 1984, occupied around 3 per cent of the labour force. Industrial employment declined from 37 to 30 per cent of total employment from 1973 to 1982.

The large share of the labour force employed in the public sector, as well as a relatively generous level of transfers from the public sector (transfers to the household sector excluding interest payments amounted to around 20 per cent of GDP in 1986), has resulted in tax pressure in excess of 50 per cent of GDP. This has, however, not been sufficient to prevent the building up of a substantial public sector debt (at end-1985 the central government net debt amounted to around 55 per cent of GDP). Relatively low domestic savings have not been sufficient to finance investments, and the resulting net foreign debt amounted to around 21 per cent of GDP at end-1986. This has in turn led to net interest payments abroad currently running at around 2 per cent of GDP.

The episode

Sweden was less directly affected by the first round of oil price increases (OPEC 1) than most other OECD countries, as the parallel increase in prices of commodities and commodity-related products, which hold a large share in total exports, protected the terms of trade. However, Sweden's export markets were hit and, furthermore, the country lost market shares at a rapid rate. These losses can mainly be ascribed to the structure of exports in terms of products and – especially – markets, as well as to the lack of consistency between domestic cost developments and the exchange-rate regime (Sweden participated in the "snake" until 1977). In the years immediately following OPEC 1 the authorities sought to cushion the domestic economy against this development by the policy of "bridging" what was seen at the time as a temporary gap in international growth. This took the form of a general expansionary policy and more targeted support to production for inventories, and led to a further deterioration in both net exports and the current account – the latter turning from a surplus equivalent to 2.8 per cent of GDP in 1973 to a deficit of 2.1 per cent in 1976. In terms of industrial production, the bridging policy

100

balanced the loss of market shares abroad, leading to a small increase (2 per cent) between 1973 and 1976.

The Non-Socialist government which came into office in 1976 after 44 years of Social Democratic rule maintained the expansionary course of fiscal policy, but the exchange-rate regime was changed in 1976-77 in response to the development in competitiveness and market shares. Within a period of one to two years the authorities devalued the krona by around 18 per cent and removed it from the European snake, seeking thereafter to stabilize the exchange rate against a currency basket. Market shares improved somewhat in volume terms following the devaluations, but far from enough to outweigh the losses in the years 1974-77; in value terms the gains were almost negligible. The continued expansionary fiscal policy together with a downturn in the domestic economy, triggered by the terms-of-trade losses following the devaluations and the abolition of subsidies for stockbuilding, led to a massive deterioration in the central government budget – from a surplus of 1½ per cent of GDP in 1976 to a deficit of 7 per cent in 1980. To some extent, this reflected the rapidly expanding system of industrial subsidies to keep ailing industries alive.

The expansionary policy was reflected in the current external account, which was further hit by the second round of oil price increases – leading to a deficit of 3½ per cent of GDP in 1980. Industrial production rebounded in the period up to OPEC 2, mostly thanks to the expansionary policies and the international upturn, and by 1979 was back to its 1973 level. Strong productivity growth – partially reflecting the legally imposed quasi-fixed character of labour input – prevented unemployment from falling below the level of 2 per cent to which it had risen in 1978.

The increasing financial imbalances following OPEC 2 triggered a more cautious line in fiscal policy, which (according to the OECD measure of change in the structural budget balance) turned broadly neutral in 1981 (reflecting the 1980/81 Budget) and was only slightly expansionary in 1982. The tighter fiscal policy was to a large extent an effect of measures on the expenditure side of the budget, with tax pressure staying around the level of 50 per cent of GDP that had been reached in 1977. To halt a slide in market shares on depressed international markets, the krona was devalued by 10 per cent in late Summer 1981. Monetary policy was also tightened in 1981 in order to respect the "norm" that had been guiding monetary policy since 1979. This norm was that the private sector capital account of the balance of payments should be non-negative; in practice, this meant that the government would finance the current-account deficit by foreign borrowings, thus implying a lower level of interest rates than if the private sector had financed the deficit.

The policy measures taken, together with relatively modest wage settlements, led to a slight fall in the current account deficit to around 2½ per cent of GDP in 1981.

The improvement on the trade balance was considerably larger, but the increasing importance of interest payments on outstanding debt, together with increasing international interest rates, masked this development, thus suggesting a shift of the current account deficit towards a more self-breeding nature. Industrial production fell in both 1981 and 1982, as market shares on the depressed international markets responded relatively sluggishly to the 1981 devaluation. Unemployment rose to – for Sweden – a record-high of 3 per cent in 1982. Reflecting this, and the interest payment dynamics of increasing debt, the central government deficit rose to nearly 13.3 per cent of GDP in 1982. The general government net financial wealth of around 29 per cent of GDP in 1976 had by 1982 turned into a net debt of around 4 per cent of GDP.

To arrest the rapidly rising public deficit, the Non-Socialist government – which as a result of considerable political turmoil had undergone frequent changes in the preceding six years – went into the campaign leading up to the election in October 1982 on a platform of fiscal austerity, implicitly giving lower priority to the goal of keeping unemployment low. Possibly as an effect of the upcoming election but also reflecting the inability of the monetary authorities to contain domestic liquidity expansion following the increasing public sector deficit, there was some currency outflow in Spring 1982, which led to a tightening of monetary policy and the introduction of new instruments to mop up excess liquidity in the private non-bank sector. Before the election, interest rates had begun to come down, but had to be raised again a week before the election to stem a capital outflow probably related to exchange-rate expectations.

On the same day as parliament adopted the new Social Democrat government the krona was devalued by 16 per cent. A few days later a comprehensive policy package was introduced, containing measures to dampen inflationary impacts of the devaluation, to give social compensations as well as to stimulate investments in infrastructure while waiting for the positive effects on activity from improved competitiveness.

Main policy considerations

The 1982 devaluation is distinctly different from other recent devaluations (but perhaps closer to the devaluations of 1932 and 1949) in its more aggressive character. Preceding devaluations were meant to make up for past differences in cost developments, and it was widely perceived – and is confirmed by OECD calculations – that relative costs after the 1981 devaluation were back to or somewhat better than the pre-OPEC 1 level. However, despite the marked improvement in competitiveness from 1977 to 1982, market shares for manufacturing exports remained approximately unchanged, while market shares had been lost at a rapid rate when competitiveness declined in the previous period. Two explanations have been put forward for the seemingly asymmetric interrelation between competitiveness and market shares. One is that, as the devaluations in 1977 and 1981 were largely defensive, i.e. making up for an adverse cost development in the past, they did not in fact provide Swedish firms with a strong competitive edge necessary to regain lost market shares. The other explanation points to the fact that profits did not recover to the pre-OPEC 1 level, and so exports may have been constrained from the supply side. Following the 1982 devaluation, profits increased very significantly and, as far as export prices are concerned, profit margins increased more than past behaviour would suggest. This increase in profits was seen as necessary – in part also to facilitate the dismantling of subsidisation schemes – by the Social Democrat government, as reflected in statements that the price reactions were up to the business sector.

It was acknowledged by all parties that the 1981 devaluation was not sufficient to halt the economy's decline, and that a sharp turn-around in policies was necessary in 1982. Although no single indicator can be seen as identifying the need for action, some were of course more important than others. On the whole it would seem that the identification of factors necessitating a change in policies did not differ fundamentally between political blocks. There was, furthermore, widespread agreement on the assessment of some constraints on economic policy. Ignoring differences between sub-periods, the policy pursued following OPEC 1, as well as terms-of-trade developments, had the effect of substituting domestic private sector demand by labour-intensive and little import-demanding public sector growth. A result of this was that real disposable wages stagnated over the period between OPEC 1 and 1982. Most parties agreed that this development had to change, and that accordingly growth had to take place mainly in the private sector and increases in tax pressure had to be avoided.

Among the most prominent factors triggering political action was the development in the public budgets. The rapidly increasing deficit and the increasing interest payments which tended to crowd out other public expenditure necessitated some action. As both political blocks ruled out significant increases in the already high tax pressure, an improvement in public finances had to come mainly from the expenditure side. In achieving such cuts, a successful devaluation strategy had certain advantages over a policy based on fiscal retrenchment combined with gradual improvements in cost competitiveness. If the aim of keeping unemployment low was to be respected, cut-backs in the public sector (or reductions in growth relative to the past period) called for a high level of activity in the private sector. The devaluation also gave a rapid improvement in public budgets via automatic stabilizers – and also provided increased opportunities for cuts in certain elements of expenditure which became less necessary. The rather dramatic increase in profitability following the devaluation made a relatively quick dismantling of subsidisation schemes for industry possible, and the improving employment opportunities reduced the need for various labour market schemes.

The balance-of-payments deficit had developed less dramatically than the public deficit, and thus appeared less out of control than the public budget. Still, it would seem to have played an important role, the simultaneous occurrence of both public and foreign deficits being seen by the government as a further indication of the need for a devaluation.

Other factors also contributed to the general picture which prompted political action. The stagnation of industrial production, which led to a fall in the volume of fixed investment in the manufacturing sector of almost 40 per cent from 1975 to 1982, was seen as a sign of erosion of the basis for future growth. In comparison with other OECD countries, Sweden had developed into a very slowly growing economy, with an average growth rate of around 1 per cent in the years 1976-82 as compared with $2^{1}/_{2}$ per cent for the OECD area as a whole.

Despite the widespread agreement on the indications of the economic malaise, the choice of strategy to combat the problems differed between political blocks, with the Non-Socialist government campaigning up to the 1982-election on a platform of fiscal austerity coupled with a wish to see a gradual increase in competitiveness as a result of lower domestic wage increases. This difference in choice of strategy would mainly seem to reflect disagreement about the controllability of the economy and the political room for manoeuvre.

A main reason why the Social Democrats distanced themselves from the strategy put forward by the Non-Socialists – although they acknowledged it as the only realistic alternative to their own strategy – was that it implied the violation of the low unemployment tradition, considered by the Social Democrats a binding constraint on economic policy. The Non-Socialists, on the other hand, did not consider the wage-reactions following a devaluation as controllable – especially not with a continued negligible level of unemployment – and thus saw no lasting positive effects. It is debated whether the differences in assessment of wage responses to a devaluation is a reflection of a general difference in the available room for manoeuvre as between a Social Democrat and a Non-Socialist government. The Non-Socialists argue that trade union behaviour is not significantly affected by the government's colour, whereas the Social Democrats believe that there is a difference – although it may be difficult to quantify. Another factor possibly increasing the Social Democrat government's relative room for manoeuvre was the political instability in the six years of Non-Socialist government, which may have increased the public's tolerance towards radical measures showing a firm determination.

As for the *timing* of the political action, it would seem that even though the problems addressed with the devaluation had been present for some time, the public sector deficit at least was developing in a way which called for rather rapid action. Other factors also contributed to make the devaluation the first act of the incoming government. The political scene had been rather unstable in the second period of Non-Socialist government and a swift action was seen as a way of demonstrating a firmer grip on developments. The three-year election cycle also called for the devaluation to be carried out early in the period so as to allow positive results to show up before the next election. In general, it was the perception that it is important for a new administration to distribute the harsh medicine quickly. The currency outflow which took place both before and immediately following the election also made a devaluation of some size (although not perhaps such a large one) more easily understandable.

The swiftness of the devaluation following the Social Democrat party's coming to power might lend some support to the thought that the decision had been taken well before its actual implementation. Indeed, the party programme presented to the 1981 congress might, in retrospect, be seen as implicitly pointing to a major devaluation. It seems, however, that the starting point for the discussion leading to the devaluation later in the year was around Spring/Summer 1982, when it became clear that the 1981 devaluation had not been sufficient to change the performance of the Swedish economy.

Assessment

The development since the 1982 devaluation has, indeed, shown an improved performance for the Swedish economy. By 1986, the current balance of payments was back in surplus – amounting to around ¾ per cent of GDP – and the central government deficit had been reduced to less than 4 per cent of GDP. Unemployment had fallen below 3 per cent after peaking at 3.5 per cent in 1983. Investments in industry increased by almost 40 per cent in volume in the period from 1982 to 1986.

A substantial share of this improvement was due to a favourable external development, notably the falling oil prices, the international recovery led by the United States and the falling U.S. dollar which both reduces the interest burden on the largely dollar-denominated foreign debt and – thanks to the dollar's large weight in Sweden's currency basket – tends to drag the krona along with it, thus giving an extra effective depreciation.

The beneficial impacts from the external environment should, however, not conceal the important role played by policy. According to the OECD estimate of change in the structural budget balance, fiscal policy has been restrictive since the devaluation – with the exception of the election year 1985 – and has been responsible for the larger share of overall budget improvement – which for the general government budget meant a reduction in the deficit from 6.3 per cent of GDP in 1982 to 0.7 per cent in 1986. This fiscal restraint has been almost entirely on the outlay side of government budgets.

Monetary policy went through some tightening in 1983 – although this was not declared until 1984 – when the norm guiding the overall thrust of monetary policy was changed so as no longer to allow any net government financing of current account deficits. Not only did the more stringent norm represent a tightening of policy, its existence may to some extent be regarded as a disciplinary element in policy formulation, providing a direct link between expansionary fiscal policy and undesired impacts on the current account and the domestic level of interest rates. The norm came under some pressure in Spring 1985, when a currency outflow led to very high interest rates. However, in retrospect, this incident may have increased confidence in the norm, as it revealed that the monetary authorities were prepared to go rather far in terms of interest rate hikes to defend it. It is debatable to what extent that outflow reflected a deteriorating current account or more speculative capital movements – or a combination of both.

The need for a considerable interest-rate differential in 1985 – when the current account was seemingly on a deteriorating trend – could be seen as a reflection of doubts about the future course of the krona. With the subsequent improvement in the current account – not least due to the falling oil prices – it was possible to reduce domestic interest rates. However, in late 1986 when oil prices bottomed out and the current account again showed signs of underlying weaknesses, interest rates had to be raised to prevent a capital outflow. This apparent tendency for increases in interest rates to be necessary whenever the current account shows weakness may owe something to cost developments. With wage increases in Sweden continuing to exceed wage increases abroad, it remains an open question how long the devaluation will remain effective. The inherent difficulties in maintaining both competitiveness and a low level of unemployment would not yet seem to have been fully dealt with, although Sweden's performance in the latter respect has certainly been better than that of most other countries.

Chapter 11

Switzerland, 1977-78:
the soaring franc

Introduction

This chapter focuses on the period of strong upward pressure on the Swiss franc in 1977-78 which was largely the counterpart, in accentuated form, of the loss of confidence in the dollar. The key issue that emerges is the extent to which the Swiss authorities were faced with a dilemma situation, and the availability or lack of instruments to resolve it.

Several features make the Swiss economy rather special. At the macroeconomic level they include: its small size – GDP represents only a little over 1 per cent of total OECD GDP; its high degree of openness – imports as well as exports of goods represent some 30 per cent of GDP; and the importance of its financial markets and international capital movements – commercial-bank gross foreign assets are the fifth largest in the OECD area. The remarkable development of the financial sector compared both with other countries and with the domestic real sector has been linked with the high saving ratio of Switzerland and its persistent tendency to exceed domestic investment; it has also reflected historical factors and the prominent role of Swiss banks and related institutions in the process of international financial intermediation. As a result, Switzerland has long been a structural exporter of both capital and financial services, the surplus on current account reflecting strong receipts on investment income and, to a lesser extent, non-factor services. In 1977-78, net investment income nearly fully accounted for a current-account surplus of some 6 per cent of GDP. The trade balance was in small surplus during this episode, but since the early 1960s the underlying position has been one of sizeable trade deficit – a point often emphasized by the Swiss authorities, along with the observation that a large proportion of capital exports typically are in long-term form and directly related to the financing of productive investment abroad. This dependence on transactions with the rest of the world has made the Swiss economy especially vulnerable to trade and monetary disturbances originating abroad and to exchange-rate variations.

During the early stages of this episode, the priorities of economic policy were to preserve the recently regained price stability and maintain a growth rate sufficient to prevent a rise in unemployment. The intermediate goal of monetary policy was to control the growth of monetary aggregates, in particular the monetary base and, through this variable, the narrowly defined money supply (M1) for which yearly targets had begun to be set in 1975. A particular feature of the conduct of Swiss monetary policy is that the National Bank, to a much greater extent than some of its foreign counterparts, believes that as long as its credibility is unimpaired the efficacy of its action can be enhanced if it fully explains what it does and why it does it. As regards exchange-rate policy, until October 1978 when it was decided effectively to put a ceiling on the Swiss franc, the authorities had been relatively flexible, responding to upward pressure essentially with administrative controls and sterilised intervention, which had not prevented a large appreciation of the SF. In addition to the specific factors and motivations discussed below, the drastic change of monetary policy and exchange-rate policy of October 1978 and, more generally, the response of the Swiss National Bank during the whole episode must be seen in the light of the rather special environment of the time and the high degree of underlying uncertainty as a result of the oil shock, the transition to generalised floating and the introduction of domestic monetary targets.

Fiscal policy did not play a major role in this episode, essentially because the Swiss authorities felt the economy was practically in internal equilibrium and that pressure on the exchange rate reflected problems and imbalances in other countries. A policy stimulus might well have quickly resulted in an overheating of the economy and new inflationary tensions, especially in view of the tight conditions in the labour market and the various impediments, not only economic but also social and political, to an increase in the number of foreign workers. In any case, it is doubtful whether fiscal policy could have been used effectively. The flexibility of this policy variable, which is typically rather low in Switzerland due to the constitutional limitations of the central government in the field of taxation and public expenditure, was further reduced at the time of this episode by a number of factors. First, since 1976 the Federal authorities, in line with the wishes of a large segment of public opinion, had sought to restrict, over the medium-term, the public sector's share in the economy and eliminate the budget deficit. Second, Switzerland seemed to have rather few viable projects for public investment. For various reasons, possibly including growing ecological concern, the programme of nuclear power plants could not be relied upon to provide a major boost to domestic demand.

The episode

The recovery from the economic recession of 1974-75 – the deepest of the post-war period – was at first hesitant but it picked up momentum in 1977, aided by strong external demand. The current account surplus, which had widened to $ 3½ billion (or over 6 per cent of GDP) in 1976, remained at around that level in 1977. The rise in prices and wages was remarkably moderate. After a year or so of relative weakness, at mid-1977 the Swiss franc began to appreciate rapidly, both in nominal and real terms. The administrative machinery for curbing capital inflows and encouraging outflows was first strengthened somewhat in the second half of 1977 and then tightened sharply in February 1978, when in an effort to stop the steep appreciation of the SF a series of special measures were taken. Among them, the discount rate, which had been lowered by half a point in July 1977, was lowered again by half a point to 1 per cent – the lowest level ever in Switzerland – and rules governing the application of the 10 per cent per quarter negative interest rate on bank deposits of non-residents were made considerably stricter. Official intervention was stepped up in the final quarter of 1977 and the authorities no longer tried to sterilise it fully. As a result, for 1977 as a whole, both the monetary base and M1 exceeded their targets, albeit only marginally. While the SF appreciated by 12 per cent in nominal terms, it was nearly stable in real terms. As noted, the appearance of a large current-account surplus in the mid-1970s had been accompanied by significant exports of long-term capital, and the deficit on the overall capital account had progressively increased. It reached nearly $ 3 billion in 1977, so that net official reserves recorded only a modest rise ($ 0.7 billion).

The economic recovery stalled in 1978, but fiscal policy remained cautious. Prices were virtually stable and the current account surplus (in dollar terms) widened further. After a lull following the measures of February 1978, the rapid appreciation of the SF resumed in May. To a large extent, this upward pressures on the SF was the mirror image of the growing weakness of the U.S. dollar: hence, it was motivated as much by disappointment and scepticism with respect to the dollar and U.S. economic policy as by confidence in the SF and the performance of the Swiss economy. Given Switzerland's price stability and strong current-account position, and in line with its traditional attraction for financial investment seeking security, the SF began more and more to play the role of a substitute reserve currency. In spite of administrative controls, funds were shifted on a growing scale from dollar assets to Swiss francs, and given the smallness of Swiss financial markets this diversification of international portfolios threatened to have disproportionate effects on the exchange rate and the Swiss economy. By end-September 1978, the Swiss franc was probably greatly over-valued: in nominal terms, it had appreciated by some 35 per cent from its level of a year earlier, and in real terms its appreciation had been only slightly smaller.

This situation led to a major shift in monetary policy. At the beginning of October 1978 the Swiss National Bank decided to give absolute priority to the objective of preventing a further appreciation of the SF over the objective of moderate money supply growth[1]. A target was set for the SF/DM rate, and to achieve it the authorities stood ready to intervene as much as required, and allow domestic liquidity to reflect this policy fully[2]. Additional administrative measures to ward off capital inflows were also taken. The strength of the authorities' commitment, and of the pressures they faced, is indicated by the ensuing increase in the monetary base by some 10 per cent in five days. The Euro-SF interest rate briefly went negative. As a result of the Swiss actions and of the dollar support package introduced by the U.S. authorities at the beginning of November, the SF declined markedly in the last three months of 1978: in nominal terms it then stabilized for over two years, while in real terms it continued to drift downward. For 1978 as a whole, net official reserves increased by the unprecedented amount of $ 7 billion, and the capital account recorded a large net inflow for the first time in several years ($ 2½ billion). The rate of growth of M1 exceeded 16 per cent, compared to an initial target of 5 per cent.

In early 1979, the Swiss National Bank was able to sell dollars and reduce domestic liquidity somewhat. "Carter notes" (U.S. Treasury securities denominated in Swiss francs and sold to Swiss residents) also contributed to mop up liquidity since the proceeds were kept by the U.S. Treasury with the Swiss National Bank. In the spring, with more settled conditions in exchange markets and the SF as well as domestic liquidity close to acceptable levels, exchange controls began to be relaxed and the authorities, in response to the second oil shock and a resurgence of inflation, resumed a policy of money supply control. But while they succeeded in keeping the monetary base practically stable for the next couple of years, the broad aggregate (M2) continued to record a brisk and uneven growth. Economic growth resumed in 1979-80 and interest rates rose, encouraged by the authorities, who by end-1979 were faced with the problem of a relatively weak SF, rising import prices (primarily as a result of the second oil shock) and accelerating inflation. The current account deteriorated markedly and recorded a small deficit in 1980 – the first one in fifteen years – but it swung back into large surplus in 1981. High interest rates, a further appreciation of the SF in late 1981 and weak external demand resulted in a new slow-down of the economy and recession in 1982-83.

Main policy considerations

In the view of the Swiss authorities, the strong upward pressure on the Swiss franc in 1977-78 was basically a monetary shock of external origin, rather than the direct result of domestic conditions and policies which, on the whole, were deemed broadly appropriate. At first (in 1977), the authorities opted for a policy of essentially allowing the exchange rate to take the brunt, since pressure did not yet seem overwhelming or long-lasting, and there still was no acute dilemma between internal and external requirements. Given the large current account surplus, the favourable cost-price performance of Switzerland *vis-à-vis* its trading partners, and the still vivid memories of the inflationary flare-up of 1974-75, a certain appreciation of the SF – even in real terms – seemed appropriate to keep the external surplus in line with structural capital exports, avoid imported inflation and keep downward pressure on domestic costs and prices. Some administrative controls were used to discourage capital inflows and favour outflows, while sterilised intervention was relied upon to smooth out exchange-rate pressure. A first limited change in policy and priorities took place in late-1977 and early-1978 when in the face of a rapidly appreciating exchange rate official intervention was no longer sterilised and controls on capital movements were tightened sharply. Hence, the modest over-shoot of the monetary base and M1 in 1977 was largely the result of deliberate policy action. But, with more settled conditions in foreign exchange markets in March and April 1978, the Swiss National Bank proceeded to mop up domestic liquidity, a move which may have accentuated the new phase of intense upward pressure which began in May 1978.

By the Autumn of 1978, the Swiss authorities had concluded that they were facing an unsustainable situation. The relentless appreciation of the SF to what seemed grossly overvalued levels was believed to pose a serious threat to the export industries and, because of their relative importance, to the domestic economy as a whole. On the other hand, given the high degree of specialisation of Swiss industry, the threat of cheap imports seemed much less acute. In terms of indicators, the unsustainability and urgency of the situation was seen most clearly in the growing complaints from most export industries of a virtual cessation of new foreign orders – rather than in traditional macroeconomic indicators such as the trade balance or the current account which were still very comfortable. The Swiss authorities regarded the strong appreciation of the SF even against the DM as the most ominous sign, not only because Germany is Switzerland's most important trading partner but because it is its main competitor in third markets. This bilateral appreciation probably reflected not only the fact that the market for the Swiss franc is considerably narrower than that for the Deutschemark but also a perception among investors of a stronger commitment of the Swiss authorities to price stability and a larger degree of independence in the determination of their economic policy – the Swiss franc, unlike the Deutschemark, floating independently of other European currencies. The seriousness of the situation and the urgent need for remedial measures was heightened by the perception that the prospect for a co-ordinated international approach was rather poor and little help could be expected from policy changes decided by other G-10 countries.

While the Swiss franc's appreciation was fundamentally a reflection of a loss of confidence in the dollar, its momentum at that stage seemed to owe much to extrapolative exchange-rate expectations. Confronted with strong expectations of sizeable exchange-rate gains, interest rates and hence monetary policy seemed increasingly unable to affect international capital movements and exchange rates. To regain a handle on the situation, the monetary authorities had to give the market a clear and reliable idea of future exchange-rate developments. It was decided that a specific ceiling for the Swiss franc would assure a maximum of clarity, and setting the ceiling somewhat below the prevailing level might be a way to show the market that even the Swiss franc can depreciate. The ceiling was expressed in terms of the DM because, as noted, this is the single most important bilateral rate for Switzerland and the Swiss National Bank felt it could enforce it (which might not have been the case for a SF-dollar rate). To assure the credibility of the operation, unlimited intervention was pledged and the proceeds were not sterilised, thereby allowing the growth of the money supply and the degree of liquidity in the economy to be largely determined by conditions in the foreign exchange market. Obviously, the related risk of inflation could not be accepted lightly, but given the unsustainability of the situation something clearly had to be done, and the alternatives looked even less attractive: a dual exchange-rate regime, for instance, which could conceivably have been introduced under the pressure of public opinion, was believed to be totally inappropriate for Switzerland, given the lack of the complex administrative apparatus required to manage it and the prospect for a major divergence between the two rates, which would inevitably result in widespread transgressions.

Intervention was indeed massive in October 1978 but, as the continued result of their actions and U.S. measures on 1st November in support of the dollar, the Swiss authorities succeeded in changing expectations with regard to their currency. This was true in particular in relation to the DM, against which the SF has been relatively stable ever since. In early 1979, interest differentials started to play a more normal role again. By April the Swiss National Bank felt it had reabsorbed a large proportion – perhaps over three-quarters – of excess liquidity, and in view of the uncertain position of the dollar and the risk of starting new upward pressures on the Swiss franc it was decided not to reduce it further. This obviously posed a risk of inflation but, once again, given the lack of a better alternative it was felt to be a reasonable risk – especially since some of the additional liquidity might represent a currency-substitution effect, that is a shift by wealth holders from balances denominated in foreign currencies to balances denominated in Swiss francs, which would not necessarily lead to an increase in spending.

Assessment

This episode seems a rare example of a true dilemma case: an economy basically in internal equilibrium confronted with a shock of external origin – in this instance, a monetary shock affecting essentially the capital account. True, Switzerland emerged from the recession of 1975 with a current account surplus which was very large in relation to its GDP, but this had been accompanied by sizeable capital outflows in long-term form. Hence, the Swiss position was one of broad overall equilibrium, with the excess of domestic savings over investment – that is, the counterpart of the current-account surplus – being spontaneously invested abroad. The situation seemed quite sustainable, even – given Switzerland's relatively small size – from the point of view of the rest of the world. Had it not been for the run on the dollar, the diversification of international portfolios and the consequent inflow of foreign funds, pressure on the SF and/or accumulation of external reserves by the Swiss National Bank would probably have remained manageable.

The dilemma was made more acute by the smallness of Swiss financial markets compared to world markets and the openness of its economy. Moreover, the Swiss National Bank found itself somewhat isolated in its explicit commitment to fight inflation, which made the Swiss franc look even more attractive than other strong currencies, such as the DM and the yen[3]. Given the scope for international portfolio diversification, even if only a small proportion of the funds shifting out of dollar assets moved into Swiss francs, it could badly damage the Swiss economy, either because of an over-valuation of the exchange rate or because of an excessive creation of domestic liquidity. Despite their firm commitment to free trade in goods, services, and capital, and the well-known limitations of exchange controls, the Swiss authorities tried as much as possible to lessen the dilemma and insulate the Swiss economy from this foreign financial shock through administrative controls to encourage capital outflows and, above all, limit capital inflows. As this approach proved clearly insufficient, and given the growing realisation of the extent to which export industries had been hurt by currency appreciation, the Swiss authorities had very few options left by the Autumn of 1978. Setting an exchange-rate ceiling and taking a calculated risk with respect to domestic liquidity and inflation seems indeed to have been the least unpalatable solution, and it received a large degree of support in the country.

Had the Swiss authorities known of the forthcoming U.S. measures to support the dollar, their decision might have been somewhat different, but even after the U.S. package Switzerland continued to face a dilemma situation. The decision of the Swiss National Bank in April 1979 to stop mopping up excess liquidity for fear of a new uncontrolled appreciation of the Swiss franc seems to have been one of the reasons for the new acceleration of inflation which followed over the next couple of years. With hindsight, it seems that the inflationary danger of excessive liquidity was somewhat under-estimated while the risk of again losing control of the exchange rate was perhaps over-estimated. But given the limited experience with a regime of floating and with monetary targeting, the reaction of financial markets was largely unpredictable. It is also difficult to disentangle the responsibility of monetary policy, notably with respect to the reacceleration of inflation and the deterioration of the current account in 1979-80, from the effects of the second oil shock. More fundamentally, even if the episode did leave a negative legacy for a few years, it does not follow that different policies would have produced better results. In the case of a dilemma situation like the one faced by Switzerland in 1977-78, the best economic policy can do may be to minimize costs.

As for the lessons of this episode, the main one may be that being a small, open economy entails both advantages and disadvantages. Switzerland had practically no problems with its form of external equilibrium characterised by a current-account surplus matched by spontaneous capital exports. On the other hand, its explicit commitment to fight inflation proved less sustainable when this was at variance not only with developments in the United States but, in the market's view, perhaps also with the position of other countries traditionally committed to price stability, like Germany. Hence the necessity for Switzerland to align itself more closely, if not with the rest of the world, at least with a major trading partner and low-inflation country.

Notes

1. In the Summer of 1978 the Swiss National Bank had already decided to suspend its target for the growth of the money supply. Following the change in monetary policy priorities of 1st October it was further decided not to set a target for 1979. (Monetary targeting was resumed in 1980, with a target for the monetary base.)

2. The target rate or, more properly, the ceiling rate, triggering unlimited intervention was set at "well above" SF 0.80 per DM – compared to a market rate of less than SF 0.80 per DM at the time of the announcement. Intervention continued to be carried out in U.S. dollars, mainly for technical reasons.

3. The favourable inflation differential had widened in 1977 to some 3½ per cent *vis-à-vis* Germany and 5½ per cent *vis-à-vis* Japan (on the basis of the GDP price deflator).

Chapter 12

Belgium, 1981-85: restoring internal balance

Introduction

For the Belgian economy, the period 1981-86 was one of ongoing adjustment to a combination of internal and external disequilibria which had built up over the 1970s, resulting at the beginning of the 1980s in a large current account imbalance (4¼ per cent of GDP in 1981), a substantial public finance deficit (13½ per cent of GDP) and high unemployment (10 per cent of the labour force). A major turning point in this adjustment process was the February 1982 devaluation, though it was only one aspect of a comprehensive corrective policy.

In view of its high and growing exposure to trade (exports account for close to 70 per cent of GDP and 40 per cent of total supply), the Belgian economy was particularly vulnerable to external shocks, though the accumulation of disequilibria was mainly due to internal factors. Thus, at the time of the first oil shock, the structures of production and demand were ill-matched, and the ailing sectors accounted for a larger part of activity in Belgium than in its competitor countries. In addition, the pattern of trade was mainly focused on Europe, where growth had fallen behind that of world demand. But the main factor in the imbalance was steeply rising wage costs relative to the trend in terms-of-trade adjusted productivity. The economy began to veer off-course in the early 1970s with a surge in real wages, subsequently consolidated by a rigid indexation system. Because of this system of indexing of wages on prices, corporate earnings bore the full burden of the adjustment to the deterioration in the terms of trade in the wake of the two oil shocks. On top of this, social security contributions were progressively raised throughout the period to finance the improvement in social insurance cover. Over the 1970s as a whole, real per capita wage costs increased by more than 5 per cent per year.

Belgium is primarily a price-taker faced with keen foreign competition both at home and abroad and, given Belgian policy up to 1981 of maintaining the exchange rate stable *vis-à-vis* the other EMS currencies, enterprises in the exposed sector were unable to pass on their higher costs to prices. They were thus forced to seek big productivity gains and closed down unprofitable plants, so pushing up unemployment sharply. Manufacturing firms also had to accept a steep fall in their profits; this led to a greater decline in investment than in Belgium's main competitor countries, throwing the economy further off course. The crisis in the productive sector was, moreover, compounded by an outflow of foreign investment, which had played a major role in the 1960s expansion. With whole areas of activity wiped out and reduced profitability, export market shares suffered major losses despite the apparent maintenance of price competitiveness.

With unemployment mounting, relatively generous social insurance mechanisms were introduced and public sector employment was expanded. These measures buoyed household demand but at the same time meant that tax and social insurance contributions had to be raised steeply (in particular corporate taxes and social insurance contributions). These actions failed to prevent a rapid deterioration on general government account and an alarming build-up of public debt. They may also have had the effect of exacerbating labour market rigidities. At the same time, the authorities sought to use exchange-rate policy as an instrument for imposing discipline on domestic cost and price behaviour. In a very open economy where most incomes are indexed, exchange-rate policy and prices-and-incomes policy are very closely interconnected. The policy of maintaining a stable nominal exchange rate proved effective in reining back price increases but, because the process of income formation remained unchanged, it compounded competitiveness problems in that it led to a steep appreciation of the real effective exchange rate in the 1970s. Moreover, from the mid-1970s onwards, in order to achieve the exchange-rate objective, the interest rate differential with average rates abroad had to be widened, adding to the financial burden of the corporate and public sectors. It is noteworthy that, apart from the dual exchange-rate system, capital movements are not controlled in Belgium and are regulated only by way of interest rates.

The episode

The second oil shock, combined with considerable political instability, accelerated the deterioration in the overall position which had become clearly unsustainable by 1980-81 on both public finance and balance-of-payments fronts. 1980 saw a major public finance overshoot, with the deficit on central government current transactions double the initial forecast. The gap between forecast and outturn widened still further in 1981 when the total net Treasury borrowing requirement stood at 13 per cent of GDP against 6½ per cent only two years earlier. For its part, the general government borrowing requirement on a national accounts basis was at 13.4 per cent of GDP, 8 points above the European average. The widening public deficit was not matched by growth of private saving and forced the authorities to resort increasingly to money financing. The outstanding public debt rose rapidly to nearly 90 per cent of domestic output in 1981, while interest service on the public debt, at 8 per cent of GDP, was among the highest in the OECD countries, a factor that did not assist adjustment when real interest rates surged in the 1980s.

At the same time the current-account deficit widened, to 4¼ per cent of GDP in 1981. This development should be viewed against the background of a sharp drop in domestic demand (down 4 per cent) which depressed imports. But the main outcome was a rapid loss of confidence in the currency, leading to outflows of private capital equivalent to almost 5 per cent of GDP, whereas in the few preceding years these capital movements had been virtually in balance. The deficit on private sector transactions, both current and capital, was such that the public sector had to borrow massively abroad (over BF 400 billion in the space of two years, or more than 10 per cent of GDP), bringing the level of gross foreign public sector borrowing up to almost 25 per cent of GDP. The outflows of private capital put heavy pressure on the free-market exchange rate, while the National Bank intervened on a massive scale on the official market. Despite this, the franc's parity was not changed at the time of the October 1981 realignment within the EMS. The effective 2 per cent devaluation within the EMS resulting from this realignment was not sufficient to ease the pressure and, at the end of 1981, the differential between the free and official market rates was over 12 per cent.

Following the 8½ per cent devaluation of the franc in February 1982 and the accompanying Corrective Plan, foreign trade in goods and services recovered rapidly; the deficit was halved in 1982 and the account showed a modest surplus (averaging around 1 per cent of GDP) in 1983-85. The current balance was back in equilibrium by 1985 and a surplus of 2½ per cent of GDP has been posted in 1986. This recovery was undoubtedly assisted by the improvement in price competitiveness resulting from devaluation and the tough wages policy pursued in 1982-83. Relative export prices in common currency terms in fact fell by 15 percentage points between the beginning of 1980 and 1984-85. But export volumes still responded disappointingly to the improvement in competitiveness, and continued to lag behind market growth even though the loss of market shares has been reduced since 1982 compared with the previous five-year period. The recovery on current account in 1982-85 seems to have been largely due to the reining back of domestic demand, which was flat in annual average terms over the period, while running at 1 per cent on average for the EEC countries and 3 per cent for the OECD countries as a whole.

Public finance was much slower to improve and in 1986 the general government borrowing requirement was still above 9 per cent of GDP. Yet, compared with the record deficit of 1983, there was very significant progress, especially given that interest service relative to GDP rose by over 3 percentage points over the period. Excluding interest payments, the balance on general government account swung from a deficit of 5½ per cent of GDP in 1981 to a surplus of around 2 per cent in 1986. These results were achieved by raising tax and social insurance contributions, particularly the latter, as well as through major cutbacks in capital expenditure (down 20 per cent in nominal terms in five years) and a marked slowdown in current expenditure excluding interest payments. Yet progress on all these fronts was still not enough to prevent the deficit from rising faster than GDP, resulting in a continuing build-up of the public debt which, by 1986, was more than 122 per cent of GDP (around 113 per cent in net terms).

Main policy considerations

Until the end of the 1970s, economic policy was designed more to mitigate the consequences of the structural imbalances than to tackle their root causes. Indeed, until the 1980 reform, constitutional problems took precedence over economic policy. Moreover, policy makers had analysed the crisis as being primarily due to sluggish demand. The authorities hence sought to boost households' income without fully realising the deleterious consequences of this policy for the corporate and public sectors. It was also politically difficult to go against the attachment of the social partners to the bargaining process, traditionally the linchpin in wage formation. Nonetheless, from the mid-1970s onward, a number of studies, in particular by the National Bank, revealed the distortions resulting from excessive wage increases and it gradually became apparent that economic policy was caught in a vicious circle of mounting unemployment, higher public spending, heavier taxes and social insurance contributions, and loss of competitiveness. A first attempt at direct government intervention in wage-setting sparked off a political crisis in 1981. This experience led the new government formed following the December 1981 elections to ask for special powers from 1982 in order to pursue its recovery programme, allowing it to legislate by decree, with parliamentary approval deferred until expiry of the period for which the special powers were granted.

Initially, priority was given to improving the competitiveness and profitability of the business sector by way of a partial suspension of wage indexation and a devaluation, the Belgian authorities considering the latter two measures to be closely interlinked. The effects of devaluation were swifter and less deflationary than adjustment solely by reducing real wages. At the same time, suspension of indexation was a prerequisite for any exchange-rate adjustment so as to avoid triggering an inflationary spiral. Last, recourse to devaluation by a country with a traditional attachment to exchange-rate stability probably had a shock effect on the social partners and facilitated their acceptance of the corrective measures.

On 21st February 1982, the Belgian franc's central rate was devalued by 8.5 per cent against all the other EMS currencies, apart from the Luxemburg franc and the Danish krona. At the same time prices and wages were frozen until the end of May 1982. While the principle of indexation remained untouched, the normal mechanism of proportional increases resulting from the various collective agreements was suspended until 31st December 1982 and replaced by flat-rate increases for all, equivalent to the increase in the minimum wage. Effectively only half of total wages thus remained indexed. This system was extended in 1983, in exchange for the introduction of a work-sharing programme. In September 1983, full wage indexation was brought back. However, real wage increases were frozen until 1986, while a "competitiveness norm" was set, allowing the government to intervene in wage formation should wages in common currency terms rise faster in Belgium than in its seven main partner countries. This provision was in fact never applied despite a slight overshoot in 1985.

The effort to put public finance on a firmer footing was still limited in 1982-83 and mainly focused on the local authority and social security accounts. The beneficial effects awaited from the improvement in the private sector fell short of expectations and by the beginning of 1984 it was clear that the target of reducing the Treasury's net borrowing requirement to 7 per cent of GDP in 1985 would not be achieved. Henceforth the prime focus of government action was to restore public finance to health. A first major programme was adopted in 1984, instituting a special 2 per cent levy on wages and transfer incomes in 1984, 1985 and 1986. Initially estimated at BF 230 billion (net effect), or 5 per cent of GDP in 1984, the programme proved insufficient, mainly because receipts were over-estimated. A new recovery plan was hence adopted in May 1986, laying greater stress on improving the management, on a case-by-case basis, of public spending, doing away with those items that were considered unwarranted and transferring responsibility for them to other agents. These measures, totalling BF 200 billion, could bring down the Treasury's net borrowing requirement to 8 per cent of GDP in 1987.

Since the 1982 devaluation, exchange-rate policy has centred on stabilising the franc's parity within the EMS. However, the Belgian franc has in fact gradually appreciated both in nominal and in real terms since the beginning of 1984. This exchange-rate policy was compatible with a gradual narrowing of the interest rate differential relative to the main financial markets. By the end of 1987 the short-term interest rate differential with Germany was down to 3 points against 5 points in 1983. In real terms, interest rates at more than 5 per cent are still high, though very much lower than the levels of almost 10 per cent that were needed to support the franc in 1980-81.

Assessment

It appears that the particularities of the Belgian system – full wage indexation and high international exposure – sharply reduced the authorities' room for manoeuvre with respect to their foreign trade deficit. A devaluation that did not form part of a coherent policy designed temporarily to change the formation of wages and transfers would inevitably fail since it would produce only an inflationary spiral that would be relatively unaffected by the increase in unemployment. On the other hand, an adjustment based solely on lower real wages would have been slower and more deflationary. With the realisation, above all in 1981, by political and social decision makers that, without an incomes policy, the debt would skyrocket and unemployment inexorably mount, the two traditional economic policy options were temporarily abandoned: namely, the contractual system of wage determination and exchange-rate stability *vis-à-vis* the European currencies. This two-pronged measure reflected a radical turnabout in economic policy. While until that time the authorities' prime concern had been to boost households' income, the crisis was now tackled by transferring a major share of households' national income first to the corporate sector and then to the public sector.

The success of this new economic policy in improving the foreign trade balance and the corporate position is undeniable. The current balance, which posted a deficit of over 4 per cent of GDP at the beginning of the 1980s, showed a 2½ per cent surplus in 1986. However, this return to equilibrium was in large measure ascribable to the curb put on demand by incomes policy, as well as to the large differential in this area with Belgium's main trading partners. The 1986 surplus, for its part, was solely due to the improvement in the terms of trade, which for Belgium represented over 4 per cent of GDP. By contrast, the improvement in competitiveness would seem so far to have had only a modest impact on foreign trade volumes. Export performance is still hampered by the failure of the productive system to make sufficient adjustment. Indeed, while there has been a pickup in productive investment since 1984, the effort in this area has not equalled the rapid improvement in corporate performance. While the corporate sector's share of national income has virtually doubled in the space of five years (from $6\frac{1}{2}$ per cent of GDP to $11\frac{1}{2}$ per cent), corporate investment ratios improved only slowly, firms preferring initially to reduce their borrowing and increase their financial holdings and particularly their foreign assets.

It is questionable how long a recovery in profits, based primarily on direct government intervention in wage formation for almost five years, can be sustained. This phase has now ended and, as in the past, wage increases are determined by the two-pronged mechanism of increasing real wages through collective bargaining and full wage indexation. In this respect the stance adopted by the Belgian authorities is in sharp contrast with the policy of reducing indexation pursued by most other OECD countries. The return to a system that was largely responsible for the imbalances of the 1970s was motivated by the need to maintain the social consensus. In 1986, indexation helped to boost corporate profits, but it also put Belgium in a very weak position in the event of a reversal in the terms of trade. Conscious of the danger, the government lodged a bill authorising it to intervene in wage formation should exceptional circumstances put its competitiveness at risk.

While in the short run the position of the corporate sector would seem to be back on a sound footing, progress in improving public finance has fallen short of government objectives. The gradual reduction of the general government borrowing requirement is still insufficient to prevent the debt burden from automatically widening the deficit. Given the weight of the debt, and on the basis of interest rate and GDP growth for 1987, a surplus on general government transactions excluding interest payments of around 5.5 per cent of GDP would have been needed for the debt/GDP ratio to stabilize, whereas in fall it should amount to only 3.3 per cent of GDP. The authorities' room for manoeuvre on the fiscal policy front is thus still very limited, even if the scale of private saving is such as to finance the deficit without undue strain.

Despite the pick-up in the current balance and the partial alignment of the Belgian franc on the Deutschemark and Dutch guilder in EMS adjustments since 1982, agents' exchange-rate expectations do not yet appear to have fully recovered. This is reflected in the continuing interest-rate differential with those offered by other financial markets, notably Germany, a differential exceeding that of inflation. The major capital outflows that resulted in 1986 from the narrowing of the differential with Germany suggests that the monetary authorities enjoy little scope for action in this area.

While still in progress, the adjustment of the Belgian economy since the beginning of the 1980s has nonetheless been impressive. It has demanded major sacrifices by the population at large, and particularly wage-earners who have suffered a loss in net earnings, *ceteris paribus*, of over 12 per cent. Acceptance of these sacrifices has undoubtedly been facilitated by the enormous scale, at the outset of the period, of the disequilibria, which were clearly unsustainable. On the basis of general agreement on the need to restore the economy to health, recourse to special powers gave the government much greater scope for action and avoided the need to achieve consensus on each individual measure. Now that these crisis procedures are no longer warranted, it may well prove more difficult to pursue the effort of fiscal consolidation which inevitably calls into question benefits that have come to be taken for granted.

WHERE TO OBTAIN OECD PUBLICATIONS
OÙ OBTENIR LES PUBLICATIONS DE L'OCDE

ARGENTINA - ARGENTINE
Carlos Hirsch S.R.L.,
Florida 165, 4° Piso,
(Galeria Guemes) 1333 Buenos Aires
Tel. 33.1787.2391 y 30.7122

AUSTRALIA - AUSTRALIE
D.A. Book (Aust.) Pty. Ltd.
11-13 Station Street (P.O. Box 163)
Mitcham, Vic. 3132 Tel. (03) 873 4411

AUSTRIA - AUTRICHE
OECD Publications and Information Centre,
4 Simrockstrasse,
5300 Bonn (Germany) Tel. (0228) 21.60.45
Gerold & Co., Graben 31, Wien 1 Tel. 52.22.35

BELGIUM - BELGIQUE
Jean de Lannoy,
avenue du Roi 202
B-1060 Bruxelles Tel. (02) 538.51.69

CANADA
Renouf Publishing Company Ltd/
Éditions Renouf Ltée,
1294 Algoma Road, Ottawa, Ont. K1B 3W8
Tel: (613) 741-4333
Toll Free/Sans Frais:
Ontario, Quebec, Maritimes:
1-800-267-1805
Western Canada, Newfoundland:
1-800-267-1826
Stores/Magasins:
61 rue Sparks St., Ottawa, Ont. K1P 5A6
Tel: (613) 238-8985
211 rue Yonge St., Toronto, Ont. M5B 1M4
Tel: (416) 363-3171
Federal Publications Inc.,
301-303 King St. W.,
Toronto, Ontario M5V 1J5
Tel. (416)581-1552

DENMARK - DANEMARK
Munksgaard Export and Subscription Service
35, Nørre Søgade, DK-1370 København K
Tel. +45.1.12.85.70

FINLAND - FINLANDE
Akateeminen Kirjakauppa,
Keskuskatu 1, 00100 Helsinki 10 Tel. 0.12141

FRANCE
OCDE/OECD
Mail Orders/Commandes par correspondance :
2, rue André-Pascal,
75775 Paris Cedex 16
Tel. (1) 45.24.82.00
Bookshop/Librairie : 33, rue Octave-Feuillet
75016 Paris
Tel. (1) 45.24.81.67 or/ou (1) 45.24.81.81
Librairie de l'Université,
12a, rue Nazareth,
13602 Aix-en-Provence Tel. 42.26.18.08

GERMANY - ALLEMAGNE
OECD Publications and Information Centre,
4 Simrockstrasse,
5300 Bonn Tel. (0228) 21.60.45

GREECE - GRÈCE
Librairie Kauffmann,
28, rue du Stade, 105 64 Athens Tel. 322.21.60

HONG KONG
Government Information Services,
Publications (Sales) Office,
Information Services Department
No. 1, Battery Path, Central

ICELAND - ISLANDE
Snæbjörn Jónsson & Co., h.f.,
Hafnarstræti 4 & 9,
P.O.B. 1131 – Reykjavik
Tel. 13133/14281/11936

INDIA - INDE
Oxford Book and Stationery Co.,
Scindia House, New Delhi 110001
Tel. 331.5896/5308
17 Park St., Calcutta 700016 Tel. 240832

INDONESIA - INDONÉSIE
Pdii-Lipi, P.O. Box 3065/JKT.Jakarta
Tel. 583467

IRELAND - IRLANDE
TDC Publishers - Library Suppliers,
12 North Frederick Street, Dublin 1
Tel. 744835-749677

ITALY - ITALIE
Libreria Commissionaria Sansoni,
Via Lamarmora 45, 50121 Firenze
Tel. 579751/584468
Via Bartolini 29, 20155 Milano Tel. 365083
Editrice e Libreria Herder,
Piazza Montecitorio 120, 00186 Roma
Tel. 6794628
Libreria Hœpli,
Via Hœpli 5, 20121 Milano Tel. 865446
Libreria Scientifica
Dott. Lucio de Biasio "Aeiou"
Via Meravigli 16, 20123 Milano Tel. 807679
Libreria Lattes,
Via Garibaldi 3, 10122 Torino Tel. 519274
La diffusione delle edizioni OCSE è inoltre
assicurata dalle migliori librerie nelle città più
importanti.

JAPAN - JAPON
OECD Publications and Information Centre,
Landic Akasaka Bldg., 2-3-4 Akasaka,
Minato-ku, Tokyo 107 Tel. 586.2016

KOREA - CORÉE
Kyobo Book Centre Co. Ltd.
P.O.Box: Kwang Hwa Moon 1658,
Seoul Tel. (REP) 730.78.91

LEBANON - LIBAN
Documenta Scientifica/Redico,
Edison Building, Bliss St.,
P.O.B. 5641, Beirut Tel. 354429-344425

**MALAYSIA/SINGAPORE -
MALAISIE/SINGAPOUR**
University of Malaya Co-operative Bookshop
Ltd.,
7 Lrg 51A/227A, Petaling Jaya
Malaysia Tel. 7565000/7565425
Information Publications Pte Ltd
Pei-Fu Industrial Building,
24 New Industrial Road No. 02-06
Singapore 1953 Tel. 2831786, 2831798

NETHERLANDS - PAYS-BAS
SDU Uitgeverij
Christoffel Plantijnstraat 2
Postbus 20014
2500 EA's-Gravenhage Tel. 070-789911
Voor bestellingen: Tel. 070-789880

NEW ZEALAND - NOUVELLE-ZÉLANDE
Government Printing Office Bookshops:
Auckland: Retail Bookshop, 25 Rutland Stseet,
Mail Orders, 85 Beach Road
Private Bag C.P.O.
Hamilton: Retail: Ward Street,
Mail Orders, P.O. Box 857
Wellington: Retail, Mulgrave Street, (Head
Office)
Cubacade World Trade Centre,
Mail Orders, Private Bag
Christchurch: Retail, 159 Hereford Street,
Mail Orders, Private Bag
Dunedin: Retail, Princes Street,
Mail Orders, P.O. Box 1104

NORWAY - NORVÈGE
Tanum-Karl Johan
Karl Johans gate 43, Oslo 1
PB 1177 Sentrum, 0107 Oslo 1 Tel. (02) 42.93.10

PAKISTAN
Mirza Book Agency
65 Shahrah Quaid-E-Azam, Lahore 3 Tel. 66839

PHILIPPINES
I.J. Sagun Enterprises, Inc.
P.O. Box 4322 CPO Manila
Tel. 695-1946, 922-9495

PORTUGAL
Livraria Portugal,
Rua do Carmo 70-74, 1117 Lisboa Codex
Tel. 360582/3

**SINGAPORE/MALAYSIA -
SINGAPOUR/MALAISIE**
See "Malaysia/Singapore". Voir
« Malaisie/Singapour »

SPAIN - ESPAGNE
Mundi-Prensa Libros, S.A.,
Castelló 37, Apartado 1223, Madrid-28001
Tel. 431.33.99
Libreria Bosch, Ronda Universidad 11,
Barcelona 7 Tel. 317.53.08/317.53.58

SWEDEN - SUÈDE
AB CE Fritzes Kungl. Hovbokhandel,
Box 16356, S 103 27 STH,
Regeringsgatan 12,
DS Stockholm Tel. (08) 23.89.00
Subscription Agency/Abonnements:
Wennergren-Williams AB,
Box 30004, S104 25 Stockholm Tel. (08)54.12.00

SWITZERLAND - SUISSE
OECD Publications and Information Centre,
4 Simrockstrasse,
5300 Bonn (Germany) Tel. (0228) 21.60.45
Librairie Payot,
6 rue Grenus, 1211 Genève 11
Tel. (022) 31.89.50
United Nations Bookshop/
Librairie des Nations-Unies
Palais des Nations,
1211 – Geneva 10
Tel. 022-34-60-11 (ext. 48 72)

TAIWAN - FORMOSE
Good Faith Worldwide Int'l Co., Ltd.
9th floor, No. 118, Sec.2
Chung Hsiao E. Road
Taipei Tel. 391.7396/391.7397

THAILAND - THAILANDE
Suksit Siam Co., Ltd.,
1715 Rama IV Rd.,
Samyam Bangkok 5 Tel. 2511630
INDEX Book Promotion & Service Ltd.
59/6 Soi Lang Suan, Ploenchit Road
Patjumamwan, Bangkok 10500
Tel. 250-1919, 252-1066

TURKEY - TURQUIE
Kültur Yayinlari Is-Türk Ltd. Sti.
Atatürk Bulvari No: 191/Kat. 21
Kavaklidere/Ankara Tel. 25.07.60
Dolmabahce Cad. No: 29
Besiktas/Istanbul Tel. 160.71.88

UNITED KINGDOM - ROYAUME-UNI
H.M. Stationery Office,
Postal orders only: (01)211-5656
P.O.B. 276, London SW8 5DT
Telephone orders: (01) 622.3316, or
Personal callers:
49 High Holborn, London WC1V 6HB
Branches at: Belfast, Birmingham,
Bristol, Edinburgh, Manchester

UNITED STATES - ÉTATS-UNIS
OECD Publications and Information Centre,
2001 L Street, N.W., Suite 700,
Washington, D.C. 20036 - 4095
Tel. (202) 785.6323

VENEZUELA
Libreria del Este,
Avda F. Miranda 52, Aptdo. 60337,
Edificio Galipan, Caracas 106
Tel. 951.17.05/951.23.07/951.12.97

YUGOSLAVIA - YOUGOSLAVIE
Jugoslovenska Knjiga, Knez Mihajlova 2,
P.O.B. 36, Beograd Tel. 621.992

Orders and inquiries from countries where
Distributors have not yet been appointed should be
sent to:
OECD, Publications Service, 2, rue André-Pascal,
75775 PARIS CEDEX 16.

Les commandes provenant de pays où l'OCDE n'a
pas encore désigné de distributeur peuvent être
adressées à :
OCDE, Service des Publications. 2, rue André-
Pascal, 75775 PARIS CEDEX 16.
71602-03-1988

OECD PUBLICATIONS, 2, rue André-Pascal, 75775 PARIS CEDEX 16 - No. 44363 1988
PRINTED IN FRANCE
(11 88 01 1) ISBN 92-64-13099-3

Why Economic Policies Change Course

ELEVEN CASE STUDIES

DEVELOPMENT

Pursuant to article 1 of the Convention signed in Paris on 14th December, 1960, and which came into force on 30th September, 1961, the Organisation for Economic Co-operation and Development (OECD) shall promote policies designed:

- to achieve the highest sustainable economic growth and employment and a rising standard of living in Member countries, while maintaining financial stability, and thus to contribute to the development of the world economy;
- to contribute to sound economic expansion in Member as well as non-member countries in the process of economic development; and
- to contribute to the expansion of world trade on a multilateral, non-discriminatory basis in accordance with international obligations.

The original Member countries of the OECD are Austria, Belgium, Canada, Denmark, France, the Federal Republic of Germany, Greece, Iceland, Ireland, Italy, Luxembourg, the Netherlands, Norway, Portugal, Spain, Sweden, Switzerland, Turkey, the United Kingdom and the United States. The following countries acceded subsequently through accession at the dates hereafter: Japan (28th April, 1964), Finland (28th January, 1969), Australia (7th June, 1971) and New Zealand (29th May, 1973).

The Socialist Federal Republic of Yugoslavia takes part in some of the work of the OECD (agreement of 28th October, 1961).

Publié en français sous le titre:

CHANGEMENT DE CAP EN
POLITIQUE ÉCONOMIQUE
ONZE ETUDES DE CAS